Iron Goddess: Mastering Women's Bodybuilding

A Comprehensive Guide to Nutrition, Training, and
Mental Empowerment in Women's Bodybuilding

SOUTHERLAND | COPYRIGHT 2023

Contents

Part 1: Overview

Unleashing Strength - Female Empowerment Through Bodybuilding

In a world where the narratives of strength and femininity are often seen as divergent, the realm of female bodybuilding stands as a testament to their powerful convergence. This introduction sets the stage for a journey into the heart of female empowerment through the lens of bodybuilding, a sport that has long been a battleground for challenging stereotypes and redefining the essence of strength in a woman.

Bodybuilding, traditionally dominated by men, has witnessed a remarkable transformation with the rising tide of female athletes who are not just participating but excelling and redefining what it means to be strong. This book delves into how female bodybuilding has become a platform for empowerment, offering women a unique avenue to assert their physical capabilities, mental resilience, and to take control of their narratives in a society that often imposes limiting beliefs.

We will explore how the discipline of bodybuilding goes beyond the pursuit of physical aesthetics. It's a journey of self-discovery, mental fortitude, and the breaking of barriers. From the meticulous sculpting of muscles to the strategic planning of diets and workouts, female bodybuilding embodies a dedication that transcends gym walls, influencing every aspect of life. It's about embracing one's power, challenging the status quo, and the relentless pursuit of personal goals.

In these pages, we celebrate the stories of women who have paved the way in the sport, defying expectations and inspiring a new generation. We confront the stereotypes and societal pressures that female bodybuilders face and offer insights into how these challenges are overcome with grace and strength. We also provide practical guidance for those embarking on this journey, from training and nutrition to mental health and community building.

This book is not just for those who live and breathe bodybuilding; it's for anyone who seeks to understand the transformative power of this sport in empowering women. It's for those who wish to draw inspiration from the discipline, commitment, and resilience that define female bodybuilders. As we turn these pages, we embark on a journey of empowerment, where every rep, every meal, and every competition is a step towards shattering glass ceilings and building a legacy of strength and empowerment.

Foundations of Female Bodybuilding

Female bodybuilding, as a distinct and formidable segment of athletic competition, represents not merely a showcase of physical prowess but a story of evolution, defiance, and empowerment. Tracing its roots, the genesis of female bodybuilding can be observed in the broader context of the history of physical culture, a narrative deeply intertwined with societal perceptions of femininity and strength. Unlike its male counterpart, which enjoyed prominence and acceptance from its inception, female bodybuilding had to navigate a labyrinth of societal norms and gender biases to claim its rightful place in the world of competitive sports.

The journey of female bodybuilding began in earnest in the late 1970s, a period that saw a seismic shift in societal attitudes towards women's roles both in and out of the sporting arena. Prior to this era, the concept of women engaging in muscle-building activities was met with a mix of skepticism and outright opposition. The prevailing societal norms dictated a certain aesthetic and physicality for women, one that did not include the muscularity and strength that bodybuilding embodies. It was in this climate that the pioneers of female bodybuilding emerged, women who not only had to fight against their physical limitations but also against entrenched stereotypes.

The early 1980s marked a watershed moment with the introduction of the first official female bodybuilding competitions. These events were groundbreaking, providing a platform for women to display their muscular development and athletic prowess. The inaugural contests, though rudimentary compared to today's standards, were revolutionary. They challenged the prevailing notions of femininity and opened the door for future generations of female bodybuilders. The athletes who graced these early stages were not just competitors; they were trailblazers, setting the foundation for a sport that would grow in popularity and sophistication.

As the sport evolved, so too did its participants. The female bodybuilders of the 1980s and 1990s began to push the boundaries of muscular development and athleticism. They trained with an intensity and dedication that rivaled, and often surpassed, their male counterparts. This era saw the rise of iconic figures, women who became synonymous with the sport and who inspired countless others to follow in their footsteps. Their legacy was not just in the titles they won or the records they set, but in the barriers they broke down in the pursuit of athletic excellence.

In tandem with the evolution of its athletes, the sport of female bodybuilding itself underwent significant changes. Categories were introduced to accommodate the diverse range of physiques and athletic goals. These categories, ranging from bikini and fitness to physique and bodybuilding, allowed for a broader participation base. They provided opportunities for women with different body types and training objectives to compete, thereby expanding the sport's appeal and inclusivity.

In recent years, female bodybuilding has enjoyed a resurgence in popularity, thanks in part to a renewed interest in health and fitness across the globe. Social media platforms have played a pivotal role in this revival, offering female bodybuilders a medium to showcase their hard work and dedication, and to inspire a new generation of athletes. The current state of female bodybuilding is characterized by a level of diversity and sophistication that would have been unimaginable in its early days. Today's female bodybuilders come from all walks of life, each bringing their unique story to the stage, and in doing so, enriching the tapestry of the sport.

The history of female bodybuilding is more than a chronicle of a sport; it is a narrative of struggle, perseverance, and triumph. It is a story of individuals who dared to defy convention and in doing so, redefined the boundaries of strength and femininity. As the sport continues to evolve, it remains a beacon of empowerment and a testament to the indomitable spirit of its athletes. Female bodybuilding, in all its forms, is not just a display of physical strength and aesthetic beauty; it is a celebration of human potential, a tribute to those who dare to dream and have the courage to pursue those dreams against all odds.

Breaking Stereotypes

The world of female bodybuilding, a realm where physical strength and muscular prowess are celebrated, has long been clouded by a myriad of societal perceptions and stereotypes. These notions, deeply ingrained in the fabric of societal norms, have historically painted female bodybuilding in a light that oscillates between admiration and disapproval, often tipping towards the latter. The origins of these stereotypes are rooted in traditional views of femininity and the roles ascribed to women, views that have, for centuries, favored delicacy and restraint over strength and muscularity. The impact of these stereotypes on athletes is profound, influencing not only their reception in the world of sports but also their personal journeys and self-perception.

The challenges female bodybuilders face are multifaceted. One of the most significant is the criticism and ridicule often directed at them. Their muscular bodies, which symbolize strength and dedication to their sport, are frequently deemed unattractive or unfeminine by mainstream societal standards. Such perceptions can lead to negative comments and judgments, impacting the athletes both personally and professionally.

The media's portrayal of female bodybuilders also plays a crucial role in perpetuating these stereotypes. Instead of highlighting their athletic achievements, dedication, and discipline, media coverage often focuses on their physical appearance in a way that emphasizes their deviation from traditional feminine ideals. This type of portrayal can reinforce the notion that muscularity and femininity are mutually exclusive, further entrenching the stereotypes.

The impact of these stereotypes is far-reaching, extending beyond the personal experiences of individual athletes. It influences public perception, affecting various aspects of the sport, from sponsorship opportunities to media coverage. Female bodybuilders often find themselves undervalued and underrepresented, with their accomplishments receiving less recognition and celebration compared to their male counterparts. This not only affects the athletes' careers and opportunities but also the overall growth and acceptance of female bodybuilding as a legitimate and respected sport.

This cycle of undervaluation and underrepresentation, fueled by persistent stereotypes, is detrimental to the progress and development of female bodybuilding. It hinders the sport's ability to attract new talent, receive adequate sponsorship and media attention, and gain the respect it deserves. Breaking this cycle is crucial for the future of female bodybuilding, requiring a collective effort to change perceptions, celebrate athletic achievements regardless of gender, and recognize the strength and dedication of female bodybuilders as worthy of admiration and respect.

Despite these challenges, female bodybuilders have played a pivotal role in challenging and overcoming these stereotypes. Through their dedication and success, they have gradually helped reshape societal norms and perceptions. They have shown that strength and femininity are not mutually exclusive and that the muscular female body can be a symbol of beauty, power, and resilience. Their presence in the sport has also opened the door for more women to embrace strength training, transforming it from a male-dominated activity to one in which women actively participate and excel.

The importance of overcoming these stereotypes cannot be overstated. It is a matter not just of fairness to the athletes but of promoting gender equality in sports. The story of female bodybuilding is, in many ways, a microcosm of the broader struggle for women's rights and recognition. By challenging traditional norms and showcasing the diversity of female strength and beauty, female bodybuilders contribute to a more inclusive and equitable sporting world.

Setting Goals and Getting Started

Embarking on a bodybuilding journey is akin to embarking on a voyage of self-discovery and transformation. For beginners, the initial stages are crucial in setting the trajectory for success, whether the goal is competitive bodybuilding or personal fitness. The foundational step in this journey is setting realistic and achievable goals. This aspect cannot be overstressed, as it forms the bedrock upon which the entire bodybuilding endeavor is built. Goals provide direction, motivation, and a benchmark against which progress can be measured. However, these goals must be realistic, taking into account individual circumstances, physical capabilities, and lifestyle considerations. A goal that is too ambitious may lead to disappointment and disillusionment, while one that is too modest may fail to provide sufficient challenge and motivation.

Understanding body types is another fundamental concept for beginners. The recognition that bodies respond differently to training and diet is vital. There are generally three body types - ectomorph, mesomorph, and endomorph - each with its unique characteristics and responses to bodybuilding practices. An ectomorph, characterized by a lean and long physique, may struggle to gain muscle and might require a more intense focus on mass-building exercises and a calorie-rich diet. Mesomorphs, with their naturally athletic build, may find it easier to gain muscle and lose fat. Endomorphs, tending towards rounder and fuller physiques, might need to focus more on fat loss and muscle toning. Understanding one's body type aids in tailoring training and nutrition plans for optimal results.

Creating a starter workout routine is another pivotal step for beginners. This routine should balance various types of exercises - including weightlifting, cardio, and flexibility workouts - to create a holistic approach to bodybuilding. For those new to the sport, the emphasis should be on learning correct form and technique rather than lifting heavy weights. This approach helps in building a solid foundation and reducing the risk of injury. Additionally, the workout routine should be varied and progressive, gradually increasing in intensity and complexity to continue challenging the body and promoting growth.

Consistency and patience are the cornerstones of success in bodybuilding. Muscle growth and body transformation do not happen overnight. They require consistent effort over time. It is important for beginners to understand that there will be periods of plateau, where progress seems to stall. These periods are a normal part of the bodybuilding journey. Patience during these times is crucial, as is the willingness to adapt and adjust training and dietary strategies. Consistency in training, adherence to dietary plans, and regular monitoring of progress against set goals will yield results, albeit gradually.

Fundamental Training Techniques

In the pursuit of bodybuilding, whether for competitive arenas or personal fitness, mastering fundamental training techniques is paramount. This chapter serves as an essential guide, introducing core exercises that form the bedrock of female bodybuilding. For beginners especially, understanding and executing these exercises with correct form and technique is critical, not only for effective muscle development but also for preventing injuries.

At the outset of a bodybuilding regimen, one must appreciate the importance of a balanced workout that targets all major muscle groups. This approach ensures comprehensive muscular development and symmetry, factors that are crucial in bodybuilding. The major muscle groups include the chest, back, arms (biceps and triceps), shoulders, legs (including the quadriceps, hamstrings, and calves), and core muscles. A well-rounded training program will incorporate exercises that adequately stimulate each of these groups, fostering balanced growth and development.

Strength training, the cornerstone of bodybuilding, is crucial in this context. It involves exercises that induce muscle contraction against resistance with the aim of building the strength, anaerobic endurance, and size of skeletal muscles. For beginners, strength training begins with learning the foundational movements: squats, deadlifts, bench presses, overhead presses, and rows. These compound movements are highly effective as they work on multiple muscle groups simultaneously, offering efficient and functional muscle building.

Correct form and technique in these exercises cannot be overstated. For instance, in performing squats, one must maintain a straight back, keep the chest up, and ensure the knees do not go beyond the toes. This proper form ensures that the exercise targets the intended muscle groups, such as the quadriceps and glutes, while minimizing the risk of injury. Similarly, for exercises like the bench press, the importance of grip width, wrist alignment, and controlled movement is vital. Learning and adhering to these technical nuances from the outset ingrains good habits and forms the basis for future training progression.

The concept of muscle hypertrophy, or the increase in muscle size, is another fundamental aspect that beginners should understand. Hypertrophy is achieved through consistent and progressive strength training, combined with adequate nutrition and recovery. It involves two key mechanisms: mechanical tension and metabolic stress. Mechanical tension is created through lifting heavy weights, and metabolic stress is induced through higher repetition ranges and shorter rest periods. A beginner's training program should ideally incorporate elements of both to stimulate muscle growth effectively.

Advanced Training

Transitioning into advanced training and nutrition in bodybuilding marks a significant shift from foundational practices to more specialized and intensive strategies. This transition is critical for athletes who have surpassed the beginner stage and are now looking to optimize their routines for enhanced performance and aesthetic goals. The introduction to this section provides an insight into what constitutes advanced training and nutrition, underscoring the importance of a tailored approach that aligns with individual physiological responses and specific fitness objectives.

Advanced training in bodybuilding goes beyond basic exercises and routines. It involves a deeper understanding of workout methodologies, incorporating a variety of training principles such as periodization, intensity techniques, and volume manipulation. This level of training is characterized by more complex exercises, including compound movements and isolation work, designed to target specific muscle groups for optimal growth and definition. Advanced training also requires a nuanced understanding of one's own body, recognizing how it responds to different types of stimulus, and adjusting routines accordingly to avoid plateaus and ensure continuous progress.

Progressive overload is the cornerstone of advanced training programs. It involves continuously increasing the demands on the musculoskeletal system to consistently gain muscle mass and strength. This can be achieved by increasing the weight, altering the number of repetitions or sets, adjusting rest periods, or modifying the exercise tempo. The principle of progressive overload hinges on the body's ability to adapt to increased stress, making it crucial to constantly challenge the muscles to stimulate growth and avoid plateaus.

Incorporating varied exercise techniques is also essential in advanced training programs. Techniques such as supersets, drop sets, and negatives add intensity and variety to workouts, helping to push muscles beyond their comfort zone. These techniques not only intensify the training stimulus but also help in overcoming the monotony that can sometimes accompany routine workouts. They are instrumental in targeting muscles from different angles and with varying intensities, which is key to comprehensive muscular development.

Advanced workout structures like split routines and pyramid training are particularly effective for intermediate and advanced bodybuilders. Split routines involve dividing workouts by muscle groups or movement patterns, allowing for more focused and intense training for each group. This approach also permits sufficient recovery for each muscle group, which is critical for muscle growth and injury prevention. Pyramid training, where the weight increases and the number of repetitions decreases with each set, or vice versa, is another effective method. This structure allows for both high-volume and high-intensity training within the same workout, maximizing muscle hypertrophy and strength gains.

Tailoring workouts to individual goals and changing needs is a vital aspect of advanced training. As bodybuilders progress, their bodies respond differently to exercises, and their goals may shift from general fitness to specific competitions, requiring different training approaches. Understanding and implementing customization in workout routines is imperative for continued progress. This includes adjusting training variables in response to feedback from the body, such as fatigue levels, muscle growth, and overall performance.

Breaking through plateaus is a common challenge in advanced bodybuilding. Plateaus occur when the body becomes accustomed to a particular training regimen, resulting in a stagnation of progress. To overcome this, bodybuilders need to employ strategies such as altering their exercise routine, increasing workout intensity, or modifying their diet. Periodization, which involves systematically varying training intensity and volume, is a powerful tool in preventing and breaking through plateaus. It ensures that the body is continuously challenged, facilitating ongoing improvements in muscle size and strength.

Preparation for Your First Competition

Preparing for your first bodybuilding competition is a journey filled with dedication, precision, and strategic planning. This chapter serves as a comprehensive guide for those embarking on this formidable endeavor, covering essential aspects from the selection of an appropriate event to the intricacies of stage presentation. The journey to the stage is multifaceted, involving meticulous preparation in diet, physical training, and presentation skills, each playing a pivotal role in your competitive debut.

Selecting the right event is the first critical step in your competition journey. Researching different bodybuilding organizations and understanding their specific categories and rules is essential. Each organization may have varying criteria for divisions such as bikini, figure, physique, or bodybuilding. Assessing your body type and training progress against these criteria will aid in choosing a category that best showcases your strengths. Additionally, consider the location, cost, and reputation of the event to ensure it aligns with your goals and capabilities.

Understanding the judging criteria of your chosen category is paramount. Judging in bodybuilding competitions typically involves assessment of muscle size, symmetry, proportion, and overall aesthetic appeal. Familiarizing yourself with these criteria will enable you to tailor your training and presentation to meet the judges' expectations. This involves focusing on developing a balanced physique that aligns with the standards of your chosen category.

Creating a competition prep plan is a crucial aspect of your preparation. This plan should encompass detailed strategies for diet, training, and recovery. Diet adjustments play a significant role in achieving the desired physique for the stage. This typically involves a phase of gradually reducing body fat while preserving muscle mass, known as cutting, which requires a carefully calibrated diet and cardiovascular regimen. Water manipulation techniques are also employed in the final week leading up to the competition, known as peak week, to enhance muscle definition and vascularity. However, such techniques should be approached with caution and knowledge, as they can affect health and performance.

Stage presentation is another critical aspect of competition preparation. This includes mastering the art of posing, which is crucial for effectively showcasing your physique. Posing requires practice and often professional guidance to ensure each pose highlights your strengths and conforms to the category's requirements. Tanning is also an essential element, as the right tan can enhance muscle definition and stage presence. Additionally, costume selection, including the choice of posing trunks or bikinis and accessories, should align with competition regulations and complement your physique.

Competing in Amateur Bodybuilding

Competing in amateur bodybuilding represents a crucial phase in the journey of a bodybuilding enthusiast aspiring to reach professional status. This chapter navigates through the multifaceted world of amateur bodybuilding competitions, offering insights that are pivotal for anyone looking to make their mark in this competitive arena. Understanding how to select the right events, grasping the nuances of competition formats, and effectively navigating the amateur bodybuilding scene are all integral steps towards achieving success and recognition.

The selection of appropriate events is a foundational step in an amateur bodybuilder's career. It involves considering factors such as the level of competition, geographic location, associated costs, and the reputation of the organizing bodies. Beginners might opt for local or regional competitions as a starting point, which offer a glimpse into the competitive environment with relatively less pressure. As one gains experience and confidence, progressing to larger, more prestigious events becomes a natural trajectory. The choice of events should align not only with one's competitive readiness but also with long-term career goals.

Understanding the competition formats is essential for any amateur bodybuilder. Different organizations may have varied rules, posing requirements, and judging criteria. Some may place a greater emphasis on muscularity, while others might prioritize symmetry and aesthetics. Familiarizing oneself with these formats through thorough research, attending events as a spectator, or seeking advice from experienced competitors can provide invaluable insights. This knowledge allows competitors to tailor their training and presentation to meet specific judging standards, thus enhancing their chances of success.

Navigating the amateur bodybuilding scene requires a strategic approach. Maximizing exposure is about more than just participating in competitions; it involves showcasing one's personality, physique, and potential to the fullest. Each competition should be viewed as an opportunity to learn and grow, taking constructive feedback from judges and peers to refine one's approach. Documenting and sharing one's journey through social media and bodybuilding forums can also augment visibility and create a personal brand.

Networking within the bodybuilding community is another key aspect. Building relationships with fellow competitors, coaches, judges, and event organizers can open doors to new opportunities and provide access to valuable resources and information. Networking can lead to mentorship, where experienced professionals can offer guidance, training tips, and career advice. Mentorship can be a game-changer, offering insights that only come with experience and can significantly accelerate a competitor's development.

Transitioning from Amateur to Pro

The transition from amateur to professional status in bodybuilding is a pivotal and transformative phase in an athlete's career. This chapter is dedicated to demystifying the criteria and processes involved in ascending to the professional ranks, a milestone that signifies not only a higher level of recognition but also an escalation in competition intensity, discipline, and commitment. Understanding the pathway to earning professional status, excelling in pro-qualifying events, and embracing the increased demands and responsibilities that come with being a professional bodybuilder are key elements that this chapter will explore.

Earning professional status in bodybuilding is typically achieved through excelling in pro-qualifying events. These events are often organized by reputed bodybuilding organizations and are the gateways to receiving a professional card. The criteria for qualification can vary between organizations but generally involve placing in top positions at recognized competitions. Success in these events demands an exceptional level of physical conditioning, presentation, and adherence to the judging criteria specific to the organization.

Strategies for excelling in pro-qualifying events involve meticulous preparation, both in terms of physical training and mental readiness. This preparation includes refining one's physique to align with the standards of professional bodybuilding, which often demands a greater level of muscle mass, definition, and symmetry compared to the amateur level. Additionally, athletes must hone their posing skills, as stage presentation is a critical component evaluated by judges. Mental preparation is equally vital, as the pressure and competition intensity at pro-qualifying events are significantly higher.

Building a compelling portfolio is another important aspect of transitioning to professional status. This portfolio showcases an athlete's achievements, physique development, and potential as a professional bodybuilder. It may include competition history, photographs, videos of training sessions or competitions, and any media coverage or sponsorships. A well-crafted portfolio can be instrumental in attracting sponsorships, endorsements, and invitations to prestigious competitions, all of which are crucial for a professional bodybuilder's career growth.

Understanding the demands and responsibilities of a professional bodybuilder is crucial. Turning pro is not merely a change in status; it's a commitment to a lifestyle where the stakes are higher, and the expectations are more significant. Professional bodybuilders are expected to maintain an elite level of physical conditioning year-round, participate in high-profile competitions, and often engage with the bodybuilding community, whether through mentorship, coaching, or social media engagement.

The transition also brings new opportunities and challenges. The opportunity to compete against the elite, increased media exposure, and potential financial gains through sponsorships and endorsements are some of the perks. However, these come with challenges such as intensified competition, greater scrutiny, and the need for continuous self-improvement both in terms of physique and professional conduct.

Life as a Professional Bodybuilder

The life of a professional female bodybuilder is a multifaceted and dynamic journey that extends beyond the gym and the competitive stage. This chapter delves into the various aspects that constitute the lifestyle of a professional bodybuilder, from the intricacies of securing sponsorships and managing media relations to the nuances of building a personal brand and navigating the business side of the sport. Understanding these elements is crucial for any female athlete aiming to not only succeed in competitions but also to maintain a sustainable and rewarding career over time.

Securing sponsorships is a critical aspect of a professional bodybuilder's career. Sponsorships can provide financial support, access to high-quality supplements and gear, and opportunities for broader exposure in the industry. To attract and secure sponsorships, athletes must demonstrate not only physical excellence but also marketability. This involves building a strong competitive record, maintaining a professional image, and engaging with the bodybuilding community and potential sponsors through social media and public appearances. Crafting compelling sponsorship proposals and learning to negotiate terms that benefit both the athlete and the sponsor are essential skills in this process.

Managing media relations is another integral part of a professional bodybuilder's life. Media exposure can significantly enhance an athlete's profile, leading to more opportunities in and out of the sport. Effective media engagement involves developing communication skills, understanding how to present oneself in interviews and public appearances, and leveraging social media platforms to reach a wider audience. Building a positive relationship with the media requires consistency, authenticity, and a strategic approach to public relations.

Building a personal brand is about creating a unique identity that resonates with fans, sponsors, and the bodybuilding community. A strong personal brand can differentiate an athlete in a competitive field, opening doors to various opportunities such as guest appearances, seminars, and even entrepreneurial ventures. Brand building involves understanding one's strengths, values, and unique attributes and conveying them consistently across all platforms and interactions. It's about creating a narrative that connects with people and positions the athlete as a relatable and inspirational figure.

The business side of professional bodybuilding encompasses financial management, contract negotiations, and career planning. Navigating this aspect requires a sound understanding of financial principles to manage earnings, investments, and expenses effectively. Athletes must also be adept at contract negotiations, understanding their worth and advocating for terms that reflect their value and contributions to the sport. Planning for a sustainable career involves diversifying income streams, continuous self-improvement, and preparing for life after competitive bodybuilding.

Balancing Bodybuilding and Life

Achieving a harmonious balance between the rigorous demands of bodybuilding and the multifaceted aspects of personal life is a challenge that every bodybuilder faces. This chapter focuses on strategies and practices that enable bodybuilders to maintain this delicate equilibrium. Balancing the intense requirements of training and competition with the responsibilities and joys of personal life, including relationships, family commitments, and other life obligations, is not just crucial for mental and emotional well-being, but it also significantly impacts athletic performance.

The first step in achieving this balance is effective time management. Bodybuilders must develop skills to efficiently allocate time to training, nutrition, rest, and recovery, while also dedicating adequate time to personal and professional commitments. This might involve creating structured schedules that clearly delineate time for workouts, meal preparation, work, family, and leisure activities. Time management also requires the ability to be flexible and adaptive, as unexpected personal commitments or changes in training schedules can occur.

Setting priorities is another key aspect of balancing bodybuilding and life. It requires an honest assessment of what is truly important and what can be compromised or sacrificed, both in the short term and long term. This might mean prioritizing training and diet over social activities during competition preparation or conversely, prioritizing family events or personal relationships during the off-season. The ability to set and adhere to these priorities, while also being open to reassess and adjust them as circumstances change, is essential for maintaining a balanced approach to life and bodybuilding.

Finding support systems plays a crucial role in achieving balance. Support can come in various forms - from family members who understand and accommodate the bodybuilder's schedule and dietary needs, to fellow athletes and coaches who provide guidance and motivation. Engaging with a community of like-minded individuals, whether in a gym setting or online forums, can offer a sense of belonging and understanding. Professional support, such as from nutritionists, therapists, or life coaches, can also be invaluable in navigating the challenges of balancing a demanding sport with personal life.

Balancing bodybuilding with life also involves recognizing the need for downtime and relaxation. Rest and recovery are as important for muscle growth and performance as they are for mental health. Engaging in activities outside of bodybuilding, whether hobbies, relaxation techniques, or spending time with loved ones, can provide mental respite and prevent burnout. It's important for bodybuilders to remember that taking time off from training or dieting does not equate to a lack of dedication, but rather it's a crucial component of a sustainable and healthy approach to the sport.

Women's Health and Bodybuilding

The realm of female bodybuilding presents unique health concerns and physiological considerations that are paramount for the well-being and performance of athletes. This chapter delves into these aspects, specifically focusing on how the menstrual cycle impacts training, the nutritional needs vital for bone health, the management of hormonal changes including menopause, and strategies for maintaining a healthy reproductive system alongside the demands of intense bodybuilding training.

Understanding the menstrual cycle's effect on training and performance is crucial for female bodybuilders. The menstrual cycle can influence energy levels, mood, and even pain tolerance, all of which can impact training efficacy. For instance, some athletes may experience increased strength and energy during the follicular phase of their cycle, making it an optimal time for intense training sessions. Conversely, during the luteal phase, some may feel more fatigued and less able to handle high-intensity workouts. Recognizing these patterns allows female bodybuilders to tailor their training programs to align with their cycle, thus optimizing performance and recovery.

Nutrition plays a pivotal role in supporting the unique physiological needs of female bodybuilders, particularly concerning bone health. The high physical demands of bodybuilding, coupled with dietary restrictions that often accompany competition preparation, can put female athletes at risk for decreased bone density. Ensuring adequate intake of calcium and vitamin D is essential for maintaining bone strength. This might involve incorporating calcium-rich foods like dairy products, leafy greens, and fortified foods into the diet, along with appropriate vitamin D supplementation, especially in regions with limited sunlight exposure.

Hormonal changes, particularly during menopause, present another significant consideration for female bodybuilders. Menopause can lead to a decrease in muscle mass and bone density and an increase in body fat distribution. Managing these changes may require adjustments in training and nutrition, such as increased focus on resistance training to maintain muscle mass and bone density, and dietary modifications to address changes in metabolic rate. Hormone replacement therapy (HRT) can also be a consideration, but it should be discussed thoroughly with healthcare professionals, weighing the benefits and potential risks.

Maintaining a healthy reproductive system is essential for female bodybuilders, especially given the intense physical and dietary regimens involved in the sport. This involves ensuring a balanced diet that supports reproductive health, avoiding overly restrictive diets that can lead to amenorrhea (absence of menstruation), and monitoring for signs of relative energy deficiency in sport (RED-S), which can have long-term health implications. Regular medical check-ups, open communication with healthcare providers, and a willingness to adjust training and nutrition programs are key to preserving reproductive health.

Weight Management and Body Composition

Effective weight management and body composition are pivotal in the sport of bodybuilding, where success is often measured not just by strength but also by aesthetic appeal. This chapter delves into the science and strategies behind managing weight and body composition effectively, an aspect crucial for both competitive success and overall health. It covers the intricacies of bulking (gaining muscle mass), cutting (reducing body fat while preserving muscle), and maintaining weight. Additionally, this chapter explores the methods for measuring and tracking body composition changes, adjusting nutrition and training to suit different phases of bodybuilding, and the psychological aspects related to body image and a healthy relationship with food.

Bulking and cutting are phases that require different nutritional and training approaches. During the bulking phase, the focus is on gaining muscle mass, which typically involves a caloric surplus – consuming more calories than burned. This phase requires a diet rich in proteins to support muscle growth, along with sufficient carbohydrates and fats to provide energy for intense training sessions. The training regimen during bulking is usually centered around heavy weightlifting to stimulate muscle hypertrophy.

In contrast, the cutting phase aims to reduce body fat while maintaining as much muscle mass as possible. This phase involves creating a caloric deficit, where fewer calories are consumed than expended. The diet during cutting is high in protein to aid muscle retention and carefully monitored for caloric intake. Cardiovascular exercises often become more prominent in training routines to aid in fat loss.

Maintaining weight, or the maintenance phase, is about finding a balance between caloric intake and expenditure to keep the body at a steady weight. This phase is crucial for giving the body a break from the extreme demands of bulking and cutting and can also be a time to focus on improving specific aspects of one's physique or performance.

Understanding body composition is crucial in bodybuilding. Body composition refers to the proportion of fat, muscle, and other tissues in the body. Techniques to measure body composition include skinfold measurements, bioelectrical impedance analysis (BIA), and dual-energy X-ray absorptiometry (DEXA) scans. Tracking changes in body composition over time can provide valuable insights into the effectiveness of training and nutrition programs and help in making informed adjustments.

The psychological aspects of weight management and body composition are as significant as the physical aspects. Bodybuilders, particularly those in competitive circuits, can face immense pressure to achieve and maintain a certain physique, which can lead to unhealthy relationships with food and body image. Issues such as body dysmorphia, where there is a distorted perception of one's body despite being lean and muscular, can arise. It's important for bodybuilders to develop a healthy relationship with food, seeing it as fuel for performance and health rather than just a tool for altering body composition.

The Psychology of Bodybuilding

The realm of female bodybuilding is not only a test of physical strength and endurance but also a significant psychological endeavor. This chapter explores the unique psychological challenges and pressures that female bodybuilders face, such as coping with pervasive stereotypes, body shaming, and societal expectations. It delves into strategies for cultivating a positive self-image, managing the mental stress associated with competition, and the importance of fostering a supportive community. Additionally, the role of mental health professionals in assisting athletes to navigate these challenges is examined, highlighting the importance of mental well-being in the pursuit of bodybuilding.

Female bodybuilders often confront stereotypes and biases that challenge traditional notions of femininity and beauty. These stereotypes can lead to body shaming and negative commentary, both from within and outside the bodybuilding community. Coping with such challenges requires a resilient mindset. Building a positive self-image involves focusing on personal goals, achievements, and the strength (both physical and mental) that bodybuilding cultivates. Female bodybuilders are encouraged to redefine beauty and strength on their terms, distancing their self-worth from societal expectations.

The mental stress of competition is another significant aspect that female bodybuilders must manage. The pressure to perform, along with the intense scrutiny of judges and audiences, can be overwhelming. Strategies to deal with this stress include mental rehearsal, visualization techniques, and developing a strong support system. Stress management techniques, such as mindfulness and relaxation exercises, can also be beneficial. Building mental toughness is not just about enduring stress but also about transforming it into a driving force for success.

Fostering a supportive community is paramount in the journey of a female bodybuilder. This community can include fellow athletes, coaches, family, friends, and even fans. A supportive community provides motivation, encouragement, and a sense of belonging, all of which are vital for mental and emotional well-being. It can also be a source of valuable advice and feedback, aiding in both personal and professional development.

The role of mental health professionals in bodybuilding is increasingly being recognized as critical. Psychologists, therapists, and counselors can provide tools and strategies to help athletes cope with the psychological demands of the sport. They can assist in addressing issues such as anxiety, body image disorders, and the psychological impact of injuries. Mental health professionals can also help athletes develop coping strategies for the pressures of competition and the challenges of balancing bodybuilding with other life aspects.

Injury Prevention and Recovery

In the demanding world of bodybuilding, where the limits of physical endurance and strength are continually tested, injury prevention and recovery are crucial aspects that require careful attention. This chapter addresses the strategies for avoiding common injuries inherent to the sport, as well as effective recovery techniques to ensure long-term participation and health. It encompasses a comprehensive overview of proper training techniques, the significance of rest and recovery, dealing with overtraining syndrome, rehabilitation practices for common injuries, the role of physiotherapy, and the fundamental importance of attuning to one's body to avert long-term damage.

Proper training techniques are fundamental to injury prevention in bodybuilding. This involves not only mastering the correct form for each exercise but also understanding how to design a balanced workout regimen that avoids overtaxing any particular muscle group. Proper form minimizes undue stress on joints and muscles and maximizes the effectiveness of the exercise. This includes aspects like maintaining neutral spine positions, using appropriate grip widths, and controlling the speed of movements. Additionally, progressively increasing weights and avoiding sudden jumps in intensity can help in reducing the risk of muscle strains and ligament injuries.

Rest and recovery are as vital as the workout itself in bodybuilding. Adequate rest allows muscles to repair and grow stronger, and prevents fatigue which can lead to poor form and injury. Recovery strategies include adequate sleep, active recovery days, and incorporating rest days into training schedules. Overtraining syndrome, characterized by prolonged fatigue, decreased performance, and increased risk of injury, can be avoided by listening to the body's signals and allowing sufficient time for recovery.

For bodybuilders who do sustain injuries, effective rehabilitation practices are key to a swift and safe return to training. Common injuries in bodybuilding include muscle strains, joint injuries, and tendonitis. Rehabilitation often involves a combination of rest, modified exercises that do not stress the injured area, and gradual reintroduction to full training. The role of physiotherapy in this process is critical. Physiotherapists can provide targeted exercises, manual therapy, and guidance to ensure proper healing and to prevent future injuries.

Listening to one's body is perhaps the most crucial element in injury prevention and recovery. This means being attentive to signs of fatigue, pain, or discomfort, which are often indicators of overtraining or potential injuries. Ignoring these signs can lead to more serious injuries and long-term damage. It involves making informed decisions about when to push through a workout and when to take a step back.

Advocacy and Changing Perceptions

In the landscape of female bodybuilding, athletes not only contend with the physical demands of the sport but also engage in a broader dialogue that encompasses societal perceptions and stereotypes. This chapter explores the significant role female bodybuilders play as advocates and influencers, capable of effecting transformative changes in how society views women in the sport. It delves into the ways these athletes can leverage their platforms to challenge existing stereotypes, inspire and educate others about the nuances and benefits of bodybuilding, and foster a more inclusive and understanding community.

Female bodybuilders, by virtue of their dedication and visibility, are uniquely positioned to serve as advocates for the sport. They have the power to dismantle long-standing stereotypes that often paint a monolithic and misconstrued picture of women in bodybuilding. By sharing their diverse experiences, backgrounds, and motivations, these athletes can offer a more nuanced and empowering narrative. This advocacy is not limited to dispelling myths about physical appearance; it also extends to challenging notions about femininity, strength, and health.

Instances of successful advocacy within the sport are numerous and inspiring. Female bodybuilders have taken to various platforms, from social media to public speaking events, to share their journeys and insights. They actively participate in community outreach programs, mentorship initiatives, and educational seminars, contributing to a more informed and respectful dialogue around the sport. Through these efforts, they are not only elevating their personal profiles but also enhancing the visibility and credibility of female bodybuilding as a whole.

Community involvement is a critical aspect of advocacy. Engaging with the bodybuilding community, as well as the general public, creates opportunities for dialogue and education. This can involve participating in forums, writing articles, or collaborating with fitness organizations to organize events and workshops. Through these interactions, female bodybuilders can share their expertise, address misconceptions, and highlight the discipline, commitment, and health benefits associated with the sport.

Using one's platform effectively is also a key component of advocacy. In an era where social media is a powerful tool for influence, female bodybuilders can utilize these platforms to reach a wider audience. This involves not just showcasing their training and achievements but also sharing their challenges, insights into the sport, and advice for aspiring athletes. By doing so, they can inspire a new generation of bodybuilders and foster a more inclusive environment for women in the sport.

Pioneering Female Bodybuilders

In the world of female bodybuilding, the paths to success are as diverse and unique as the athletes themselves. This section delves into the inspirational stories and personal narratives of successful female bodybuilders, offering a glimpse into their journeys. From overcoming significant challenges to achieving remarkable triumphs, these stories not only inspire but also illuminate the varied backgrounds and paths that have led these women to excel in the sport of bodybuilding. Each of these women is a testament to perseverance, dedication, and the unyielding pursuit of personal goals.

Andrea Shaw

Instagram: @mzprettymuscle

Andrea Shaw's journey in bodybuilding is a narrative of relentless pursuit and remarkable achievement. Initiating her muscle-building voyage at the age of 17, Andrea was under the guiding influence of her mother, a nurse and a former personal trainer. This early start, coupled with a solid educational foundation with a BA in Exercise and Sports Science, set the stage for her rapid ascent in the sport of bodybuilding.

Her commitment and dedication were swiftly recognized in the competitive arena. Andrea's significant milestone came in 2018 when she earned her professional card at the NPC Nationals, a testament to her hard work and potential. Further cementing her rising status, she clinched a win at the 2018 Lenda Murray Detroit Classic, showcasing her prowess and dedication to the sport.

A turning point in Andrea's career was a pivotal conversation with the renowned bodybuilding legend Lenda Murray at the Toronto Pro 2019. This interaction inspired a strategic shift in her focus from physique to bodybuilding – a decision that propelled her career forward and amplified her success. This transition was marked by immediate and impressive achievements, most notably winning the prestigious titles of Ms Olympia in 2020 and the Ms Rising Phoenix champion. These accolades not only solidified her position in the sport but also marked her as a significant and influential figure in female bodybuilding.

Andrea Shaw's story is one of inspiration and determination, highlighting the impact of early mentorship, the importance of educational grounding in sports science, and the courage to make strategic shifts in one's career. Her accomplishments speak volumes about her talent and relentless drive, making her a role model for aspiring bodybuilders and a celebrated figure in the world of female bodybuilding.

Melina Keltaniemi

Instagram: @melinakatarina

Melina Keltaniemi, at the young age of 22, has emerged as a prominent figure in the realm of female bodybuilding, showcasing remarkable talent and dedication. Her journey in the sport is marked by significant achievements and a balanced approach to training and recovery. Melina's accomplishments are notable, particularly in major international competitions, highlighting her status as a rising star in the field.

A key highlight of Melina's career was her performance at the 2018 Nordic Elite Pro, where she secured 2nd place, demonstrating her prowess and competitive spirit. This achievement was further complemented by her performance at the IFBB Elite Pro Russia, where she earned a commendable 3rd place. These successes on the international stage were indicative of her skill and potential in the sport.

The pinnacle of Melina's achievements in 2018 was winning the title of IFBB Elite Pro World Champion. This prestigious accolade not only solidified her position as a formidable competitor in female bodybuilding but also marked her as an athlete with exceptional potential and a bright future ahead.

What sets Melina apart is her strategic approach to training and rest. She understands the importance of balancing intense training sessions with adequate rest periods, a methodology that ensures both optimal performance and longevity in her career. This balanced approach is crucial in a sport that demands both physical and mental endurance and is a testament to her understanding of the importance of holistic athlete development.

Melina Keltaniemi's accomplishments at a young age, coupled with her thoughtful approach to training and recovery, make her a notable athlete in the world of female bodybuilding. Her successes serve not only as a foundation for a promising career but also as inspiration for upcoming athletes in the sport. Her story underscores the significance of strategic training, rest, and the pursuit of excellence in competitive bodybuilding.

Monique Jones

Instagram: @fitnique

Monique Jones, an esteemed American athlete in the world of female bodybuilding, has carved a niche for herself with her exceptional skill and dedication to the sport. Her journey in bodybuilding, marked by significant achievements and a deep-seated passion for the sport, has led her to be ranked 7th on the IFBB Pro Women's Bodybuilding Ranking List, a testament to her prowess and commitment.

Monique discovered her passion for bodybuilding at the young age of 13, a discovery that set the stage for her future in the sport. Her natural aptitude for athleticism was evident early on, and it propelled her through the ranks of competitive bodybuilding. This innate talent, combined with her dedication to training and improvement, laid the foundation for her remarkable career.

A significant milestone in Monique's journey was her triumph at the IFBB North American Championships, where she competed as a heavyweight. Her victory in this prestigious competition not only showcased her exceptional abilities but also earned her the coveted IFBB Pro card, marking her entry into the professional arena of bodybuilding.

Monique's list of accomplishments is both impressive and inspiring. A notable highlight of her career was winning the 2018 IFBB WOS Romania Muscle Fest Pro, a victory that underscored her status as a leading figure in female bodybuilding. Further adding to her accolades was her performance at the 2019 Rising Phoenix World Championships, where she secured a commendable 5th place, competing against some of the best athletes in the sport.

Monique Jones' journey in bodybuilding, from discovering her passion as a teenager to achieving recognition on the professional stage, is a story of perseverance, talent, and unwavering dedication. Her achievements serve not only as a testament to her hard work and commitment but also as an inspiration to aspiring bodybuilders, proving that with passion and persistence, one can reach the pinnacle of success in the sport.

Andrulla Blanchette

Instagram: @ms.olympia2000

Andrulla Blanchette stands as a distinguished figure in the history of UK female bodybuilding, with a career spanning from 1986 to 2002 that has earned her recognition as one of the most accomplished British female bodybuilders. Her tenure in the sport is marked by significant achievements and a legacy that continues to influence the new generation of bodybuilders.

Blanchette's career highlights include major victories that showcase her exceptional talent and dedication to bodybuilding. One of her most notable achievements was her triumph at the World Games in 1993, a victory that not only underscored her skill and competitive spirit but also significantly elevated her status in the international bodybuilding community. Further cementing her legacy was her remarkable win at the Ms. Olympia competition in 2000, one of the most prestigious titles in the sport of bodybuilding. This victory placed her among the elite athletes in female bodybuilding and exemplified her outstanding commitment and prowess in the sport.

Beyond her competitive achievements, Andrulla Blanchette's impact on the sport extends to her role as a mentor and trainer. Her personal training gym serves as a nurturing ground for the next generation of UK female bodybuilders. Through her mentorship, Blanchette imparts valuable knowledge, experience, and guidance, playing a pivotal role in shaping the future of the sport. Her involvement in training the upcoming athletes demonstrates her dedication to the growth and development of female bodybuilding, ensuring her influence and legacy endure beyond her competitive years.

Andrulla Blanchette's journey in bodybuilding, marked by remarkable victories and continued mentorship, exemplifies a career filled with passion, achievement, and enduring influence. Her contributions to the sport have not only etched her name in the annals of bodybuilding history but have also paved the way for future generations of female bodybuilders in the UK and beyond.

Yaxeni Oriquen

Instagram: @yaxenita

Yaxeni Milagros Oriquen-Garcia Perez, a Venezuelan-American bodybuilding champion, has etched her name in the annals of the sport's history as one of its most illustrious figures. Her remarkable list of achievements and enduring presence in the sport exemplify not only her physical capabilities but also her unwavering dedication and passion for bodybuilding.

Yaxeni's career is adorned with prestigious titles, most notably her victory in the Ms. Olympia competition in 2005, a pinnacle achievement in the world of female bodybuilding. This victory marked her as a leading figure in the sport, showcasing her exceptional dedication, training discipline, and bodybuilding acumen. Additionally, her impressive accomplishment of winning five Ms. International titles further cements her status as a dominant force in the sport.

At the age of 54, Yaxeni's influence extends beyond her competition successes. She continues to be a source of inspiration and motivation within the bodybuilding community and beyond. Her commitment to maintaining a healthy lifestyle serves as a powerful example for athletes of all ages, proving that dedication to fitness and well-being can have a profound impact at any stage of life. Her efforts to encourage others to embrace fitness and a healthy lifestyle demonstrate her commitment not just to her own success but also to the betterment of others.

Yaxeni Oriquen-Garcia Perez, along with other esteemed athletes in female bodybuilding, represents the pinnacle of the sport. Their journeys highlight the immense physical prowess, mental resilience, and emotional strength required to excel in bodybuilding. These athletes serve as beacons of inspiration, not only for those aspiring to follow in their footsteps in the world of bodybuilding but also for anyone seeking to embark on a fitness journey. Their stories exemplify the transformative power of dedication and perseverance, offering encouragement and motivation to all who seek to overcome challenges and achieve excellence in their athletic endeavors.

Theresa Ivancik

Instagram: @tivancik_ifbbpro

Theresa Ivancik stands out as a remarkable athlete in the IFBB Pro League, marking her presence as a beacon of excellence in the world of female bodybuilding. Her achievements and rank as 6th worldwide reflect her dedication and skill in the sport. Ivancik's journey in bodybuilding is characterized by notable successes and a profound commitment to promoting and supporting the sport, particularly for women athletes.

Her performance at the 2019 Rising Phoenix World Championships, where she secured a 6th place finish, highlights her competitive spirit and prowess. This achievement is a testament to her hard work and dedication to the sport. The 2019 season was particularly noteworthy for Ivancik. Her victory at the Lenda Murray Norfolk Pro show not only showcased her exceptional abilities but also secured her a coveted spot at the Rising Phoenix World Championships. This win is a significant milestone in her career, underscoring her status as a top competitor in female bodybuilding.

Theresa Ivancik is also celebrated for her exceptional posing skills, a crucial aspect of bodybuilding that combines artistry and athleticism. Her talent in this area was recognized when she won the "Best Poser" award, a prestigious accolade that highlights her proficiency and creativity in presenting her physique. Additionally, her invitation to guest pose at the Olympia expo stage is a recognition of her standing in the sport and her ability to inspire and captivate audiences.

Beyond her competitive achievements, Ivancik's collaboration with Wings of Strength exemplifies her commitment to the broader aspects of female bodybuilding. Wings of Strength is an organization dedicated to promoting and supporting female bodybuilders, and Ivancik's involvement with them underscores her dedication not only to her personal success but also to the growth and empowerment of other women in the sport. Her efforts contribute significantly to creating opportunities and a supportive environment for female bodybuilders, helping to advance the sport and inspire the next generation of athletes.

Theresa Ivancik's achievements in bodybuilding, coupled with her commitment to promoting and supporting the sport, make her a notable figure in the IFBB Pro League. Her success at the Rising Phoenix World Championships, her exceptional posing skills, and her involvement with Wings of Strength highlight her as a versatile and influential athlete in female bodybuilding. Ivancik's journey and contributions to the sport serve as an inspiration, demonstrating the impact one can have both as a competitor and as a supporter of female bodybuilding.

Elisa Pecini

Instagram: @isapecini

Elisa Pecini, hailing from Brazil, has rapidly ascended to prominence in the bikini competition circuit, showcasing her remarkable talent and determination at a young age. Her journey in the sport is not just a chronicle of competitive victories but also a deeply personal narrative of overcoming significant challenges and emerging as a symbol of resilience and empowerment.

Pecini's accomplishments in the realm of bodybuilding are noteworthy, particularly considering her age. Her string of victories is impressive, including winning the 2018 MuscleContest Nacional Pro Bikini, the 2018 Pittsburgh Pro Bikini, and the 2018 MuscleContest Brazil Pro Bikini. These successes laid the groundwork for her most significant triumph yet - clinching the title in the Bikini Olympia category at the prestigious Mr. Olympia in 2019. This victory at one of the sport's most revered competitions marked her as a leading figure in the bikini division of bodybuilding.

However, Elisa Pecini's story transcends her competitive achievements. Her journey is profoundly marked by her battle and victory over anorexia nervosa. This personal struggle with an eating disorder and her subsequent transformation into a champion bodybuilder is a testament to her inner strength and determination. Overcoming such a challenging phase of her life to achieve physical and mental well-being is an inspiring tale of triumph over adversity.

Today, Elisa Pecini stands as much more than a champion bodybuilder; she is an advocate and a source of inspiration. Utilizing her platform, she shares her experiences, reaching out to others who may face similar struggles. Her story is a powerful reminder of the importance of a healthy approach to bodybuilding and life. She emphasizes that strength comes not only from physical training but also from a balanced and healthy lifestyle, both mentally and emotionally.

Elisa Pecini's journey in bodybuilding is a beacon of hope and inspiration, highlighting that with resilience, dedication, and a healthy approach, it is possible to overcome personal struggles and achieve greatness in the sport. Her story resonates beyond the realms of bodybuilding, offering encouragement and motivation to all who hear it, emphasizing the transformative power of sports in achieving personal empowerment and well-being.

Sarah Villegas

Instagram: @iamsarahfit

Sarah Villegas, an esteemed IFBB Pro, personal trainer, and certified sports nutritionist, has etched her name in the annals of female bodybuilding with her remarkable achievements and influence in the sport. Her journey, marked by significant victories and a dedicated approach to fitness and nutrition, exemplifies her status as a rising star and a source of inspiration in the bodybuilding community.

Villegas's win at the 2020 Olympia: Women's Physique is a testament to her skill, hard work, and dedication. This prestigious title is one of the most coveted in the sport, marking her as a leading figure in the women's physique category. Her success is further highlighted by her impressive performances at the IFBB Pro Olympian, where she has garnered both silver and gold medals, showcasing her consistency and competitiveness at the highest level.

Her career trajectory took a significant turn in 2019 when she clinched 2nd place in the Olympia Women's Physique competition. This achievement not only demonstrated her potential but also set the stage for her future successes. Villegas's journey to the professional ranks began at the Universe Championships in 2017, where she earned her pro status, marking the beginning of her ascendancy in professional bodybuilding.

Beyond her competitive achievements, Sarah Villegas is recognized for her disciplined approach to training and her extensive knowledge in fitness and nutrition. As a personal trainer and sports nutritionist, she brings a wealth of expertise, guiding and inspiring others in their fitness journeys. Her commitment to sharing her knowledge and experience is evident in her role as a Fitness Director at AFS Premier Fitness, where she continues to influence and motivate individuals to achieve their fitness goals.

Sarah Villegas's career in bodybuilding goes beyond personal victories; it encompasses her role as a mentor and educator in the field of fitness and nutrition. Her disciplined approach, combined with her dedication to helping others, makes her a pivotal figure in the bodybuilding community. As she continues to push the boundaries in her career, Sarah Villegas remains a beacon of inspiration, demonstrating the transformative power of dedication and expertise in the world of female bodybuilding.

Shanique Grant

Instagram: @therealfitnessbeauty

Shanique Grant, an American IFBB professional bodybuilder and online coach, has etched a significant mark in the Women's Physique category, showcasing remarkable resilience and determination. Her journey in bodybuilding is a compelling narrative of overcoming adversity, achieving remarkable success, and transforming challenges into triumphs.

Grant's ascent in the realm of professional bodybuilding was meteoric. Winning her pro card just four months into her competitive career is a testament to her exceptional talent and hard work. Her prowess was further solidified when she clinched the Women's Physique Olympia title at the young age of 23 in 2018, and remarkably, she repeated this feat in 2019. These victories at one of the most prestigious stages in bodybuilding not only underscored her athletic capabilities but also her mental fortitude.

The path to these achievements, however, was not without its challenges. Shanique's early life was marred by teenage bullying and health challenges, experiences that she transformed into fuel for her bodybuilding ambitions. Her journey to the sport was as much about building physical strength as it was about finding empowerment and self-confidence.

Grant's competitive record is impressive, with significant wins like the 2016 New York Pro in the IFBB Pro Women Physique category. Her resilience was put to the test in 2016 when she faced a violent attack, resulting in severe injuries. Demonstrating extraordinary strength and determination, she made a powerful comeback to win the New York Pro again in 2017, a victory that speaks volumes about her character and perseverance.

In 2020, after placing second at the Olympia, Shanique announced her retirement from competitive bodybuilding. Her decision marked the end of a remarkable chapter in her career but also the beginning of a lasting legacy. Shanique Grant's story in the world of bodybuilding is not just about the accolades and titles; it's a narrative of overcoming personal obstacles, challenging the odds, and inspiring others through her journey.

As an online coach, Grant continues to impact the world of fitness, sharing her knowledge and experience, and motivating others to pursue their fitness goals. Her legacy in the sport is characterized by resilience, determination, and the transformative power of bodybuilding to change lives. Shanique Grant's journey will continue to inspire future generations of bodybuilders and fitness enthusiasts.

Stefi Cohen

Instagram: @steficohen

Dr. Stefi Cohen, a highly renowned figure in the world of strength sports and a distinguished physical therapist, stands as a paragon of raw power, discipline, and achievement. Her remarkable journey in powerlifting is marked by setting numerous world records and her multifaceted involvement in the broader fitness and strength community.

Cohen's feats in powerlifting are nothing short of extraordinary. Her record of a 202.5kg squat and a staggering 205kg deadlift are testaments to her exceptional strength and dedication to the sport. These achievements not only showcase her physical capabilities but also her mental resilience and strategic approach to training and competition.

Beyond her athletic prowess, Stefi Cohen has cultivated a significant presence in the digital and entrepreneurial world. Her substantial social media following is a reflection of her influence and popularity in the strength community. Through her platforms, she shares insights, training tips, and motivational content, reaching a wide audience of fitness enthusiasts and aspiring athletes.

As a co-host of a podcast, Stefi provides a platform for discussions on a range of topics relevant to strength training, health, and fitness. This endeavor further amplifies her role as an educator and influencer in the field.

Stefi's entrepreneurial spirit is evident in her co-ownership of Hybrid Performance Method, a coaching company dedicated to helping individuals achieve their athletic and aesthetic goals. Through this venture, she combines her expertise in physical therapy and strength training to offer comprehensive training programs and guidance.

A notable highlight of her career occurred in 2020 when she made the strategic decision to drop to a lower weight class. This move proved to be successful as she continued to break records, bringing her total to an astounding 25 world records. This achievement underlines her ability to adapt and excel, setting new benchmarks in the sport of powerlifting.

Stefi Cohen's journey is a remarkable example of setting and achieving realistic fitness goals. Her success in powerlifting, coupled with her contributions as an educator, influencer, and entrepreneur, makes her an inspirational figure in the strength community. Her story not only motivates athletes and fitness enthusiasts but also exemplifies the impact of dedication, strategic planning, and passion in achieving excellence in the realm of strength sports.

These athletes represent not only the pinnacle of competitive success but also the sheer will and resilience needed to overcome personal and physical challenges. From Shanique's inspiring comeback to Stefi's record-setting performances, their stories are a testament to the strength and spirit of female bodybuilders, making them influential figures in the fitness community.

Explore a rewarding career in fitness with OriGym's Personal Training Diploma. Qualify in just 2 weeks and start your journey in one of the most dynamic and fulfilling industries today. Learn more about our comprehensive, CIMSPA-endorsed programs, and begin your transformation into a fitness professional.

These exceptional athletes not only represent the pinnacle of physical conditioning and competitive success but also embody the strength, resilience, and spirit of female empowerment in the sport of bodybuilding. Their journeys, marked by both triumphs and challenges, continue to inspire a new generation of women in the fitness world.

Beyond Competitions

Life for female bodybuilders extends far beyond the competition arena. This chapter explores the spectrum of opportunities and pathways that open up for female bodybuilders, especially in the context of long-term career planning and the transition into various roles within the fitness industry. It delves into the possibilities that emerge from the skills, discipline, and knowledge gained through bodybuilding, such as coaching, personal training, and entrepreneurship. Additionally, the chapter addresses the crucial aspect of planning for retirement and ways to stay involved in the sport after the culmination of active competition.

Transitioning into roles like coaching and personal training is a natural progression for many female bodybuilders. With their extensive knowledge of fitness, nutrition, and the discipline required to succeed in the sport, they are well-equipped to guide others on their fitness journeys. As coaches, they can impart not only training techniques but also share valuable insights into competition preparation, mental toughness, and the holistic approach to bodybuilding. Personal training allows for a more individualized approach, helping clients achieve their fitness goals, whether they aspire to compete in bodybuilding or simply wish to improve their health and physique.

Entrepreneurship within the fitness industry is another avenue that many female bodybuilders pursue. This can involve opening gyms or fitness centers, starting a fitness-related business, or developing a brand around fitness apparel or supplements. The entrepreneurial route offers an opportunity to leverage one's reputation and expertise in bodybuilding to build a business that aligns with personal passions and professional goals.

Planning for retirement is an essential aspect of a bodybuilder's career. Unlike many traditional careers, professional bodybuilding does not typically offer pension plans or retirement benefits. Therefore, it is crucial for athletes to plan financially for their future. This can involve saving and investing earnings from competitions, sponsorships, and other fitness-related ventures, as well as exploring other income streams that can provide financial stability post-retirement.

Staying involved in the sport after active competition is important for many retired bodybuilders. This involvement can take various forms, such as mentoring upcoming athletes, serving as a judge or official at bodybuilding competitions, or engaging in speaking engagements and seminars. Staying connected to the bodybuilding community can provide a sense of purpose and fulfillment, allowing retired athletes to give back to the sport that shaped their lives.

Global Perspectives

Female bodybuilding, as a global phenomenon, presents a tapestry of diverse experiences and challenges influenced by varying cultural backgrounds. This chapter explores the worldwide landscape of female bodybuilding, delving into how the sport is perceived, practiced, and shaped by different cultures across the globe. It examines the influence of cultural norms on training, competition, and the overall journey of female bodybuilders. Additionally, this chapter highlights the global impact of these athletes and the international efforts aimed at promoting and supporting women in the sport.

The perception and practice of female bodybuilding vary significantly across different regions. In some cultures, the sport is widely accepted and celebrated, with female bodybuilders receiving substantial support and recognition. These environments often have well-developed infrastructures for training, competitions, and athlete development. However, in other regions, female bodybuilding may still be emerging or facing cultural barriers. In such places, stereotypes about femininity and strength can pose significant challenges to women who pursue bodybuilding. These cultural nuances influence not only the availability of resources and opportunities for female bodybuilders but also the level of societal support and acceptance they receive.

Cultural norms significantly impact the training and competition experiences of female bodybuilders. In certain cultures, women face limited access to training facilities or may encounter societal resistance to their participation in what is often perceived as a male-dominated sport. These barriers can affect everything from the type of training they can undertake to the kinds of competitions available to them. Conversely, in more inclusive cultures, female bodybuilders may experience fewer restrictions and greater encouragement, allowing for a more robust development within the sport.

The global impact of female bodybuilders is profound, as these athletes often become role models and advocates, inspiring women worldwide to pursue fitness and strength training. Through international competitions, social media, and global fitness events, female bodybuilders have the platform to showcase their talents and share their experiences, transcending cultural boundaries. Their success stories become a source of motivation and empowerment for women globally, challenging stereotypes and expanding the sport's reach.

International efforts to promote and support women in bodybuilding are growing. Organizations and federations are increasingly recognizing the need for more inclusive and supportive environments for female athletes. These efforts include creating more categories and competitions specifically for women, offering educational resources and training programs, and advocating for greater equality and diversity in the sport. Collaborations across countries and cultures are also playing a crucial role in advancing the sport, fostering a sense of global community among female bodybuilders.

Steroids and Female Bodybuilding

The topic of steroids in female bodybuilding is a complex and often contentious issue, marked by a blend of historical, ethical, and health-related considerations. This chapter aims to provide a candid exploration of the role and impact of steroids within the realm of female bodybuilding. It delves into the history of steroid use in the sport, examining why some athletes turn to these performance-enhancing drugs, and the specific health risks they pose, especially to women. Furthermore, the chapter addresses the legal and ethical considerations surrounding steroids and engages with the ongoing debate within the bodybuilding community about their use. The primary goal is to offer a comprehensive understanding that aids readers in making informed decisions and comprehending the full scope of consequences associated with steroid use.

The history of steroid use in bodybuilding dates back several decades, aligning with the broader history of performance-enhancing drugs in various sports. Initially, steroids were used for their medical benefits but gradually found their way into the sports arena as athletes sought ways to improve their performance. In female bodybuilding, the use of steroids has been a particularly sensitive issue, given the potential for significant changes not only in muscle mass but also in secondary sexual characteristics.

The reasons some female bodybuilders turn to steroids are multifaceted. The pressure to succeed and compete at higher levels, the desire for rapid muscle growth, and the influence of certain segments of the bodybuilding community all play a part. However, the decision to use steroids is often made without fully understanding the health implications, particularly for women. Steroids can lead to a range of adverse effects, including but not limited to, hormonal imbalances, menstrual cycle disruptions, deepening of the voice, and increased risk of certain diseases.

The health risks associated with steroid use are particularly pronounced for women due to the way these substances interact with the female body. Steroids can disrupt the delicate hormonal balance crucial for various bodily functions, leading to both short-term side effects and long-term health issues. These risks necessitate a thorough understanding and cautious approach to steroid use, underlining the importance of prioritizing health over competitive advantage.

Legal and ethical considerations are also paramount when discussing steroids in female bodybuilding. The legality of steroid use varies by country and bodybuilding organization, with most considering them illegal and against the rules of fair competition. Ethically, the use of steroids raises questions about sportsmanship, the integrity of competition, and the message it sends to upcoming athletes in the sport.

The ongoing debate within the bodybuilding community about steroid use is both vigorous and divisive. Some argue for a more lenient approach, citing the widespread use and the potential for safe usage under medical supervision. Others advocate for strict prohibition, emphasizing the health risks, legal issues, and the need for a level playing field.

Emerging Trends in Female Bodybuilding

As female bodybuilding evolves, it is continually shaped by emerging trends and developments that influence training methodologies, nutritional approaches, and the sport's overall landscape. This chapter focuses on these evolving aspects, providing insights into the latest advancements and predicting future trends in female bodybuilding. It explores new training techniques, nutritional innovations, the rising popularity of various bodybuilding categories, and the impact of technology and social media on the sport.

New training methodologies in female bodybuilding are revolutionizing how athletes prepare and compete. These methodologies are increasingly informed by scientific research, focusing on optimizing muscle growth, enhancing recovery, and preventing injuries. Techniques such as high-intensity interval training (HIIT), functional movement exercises, and periodization are becoming more prevalent. These methods not only improve physical strength and aesthetics but also enhance overall athletic performance and reduce the risk of overtraining.

Nutritional advancements are playing a crucial role in the evolution of female bodybuilding. There is a growing emphasis on personalized nutrition plans tailored to individual metabolic rates, recovery needs, and specific training goals. The use of dietary supplements is becoming more targeted, with a focus on optimizing muscle recovery, enhancing endurance, and supporting overall health. Additionally, there is an increasing awareness of the importance of holistic nutrition strategies that incorporate not just macronutrients but also micronutrients, hydration, and gut health.

The popularity of different bodybuilding categories is expanding, reflecting a broader range of opportunities and inclusivity within the sport. Categories such as bikini, wellness, figure, physique, and traditional bodybuilding offer athletes various ways to compete based on their body types and personal preferences. This diversification is attracting a wider range of participants, showcasing different aspects of female strength and aesthetics.

The impact of technology and social media on female bodybuilding has been transformative. These platforms provide athletes with unprecedented access to information, training resources, and global networks. Social media, in particular, has become a powerful tool for marketing, personal branding, and community building. Athletes can share their journeys, connect with fans, and build their brand, while also inspiring and educating others about the sport. Technology in training equipment and apps is also enhancing the way athletes train and track their progress.

Looking to the future, it is expected that these trends will continue to shape the landscape of female bodybuilding. The sport is likely to see further advancements in training and nutrition science, greater customization in athlete preparation, and continued growth in the diversity of competition categories. Technology and social media will further integrate into the fabric of the sport, influencing training, competition, and community engagement.

The Future of Female Bodybuilding

The future of female bodybuilding stands at a dynamic crossroads, shaped by evolving trends, growing advocacy, and advancements in scientific research. This chapter offers a forward-looking perspective on how these elements might collectively influence and mold the sport in the coming years. It delves into the potential shifts in competition standards and categories, the impact of scientific research on training and nutrition, and how the changing social and cultural landscape could alter the perception and popularity of female bodybuilding.

Advocacy for inclusivity and diversity is playing a pivotal role in the evolution of female bodybuilding. As advocates push for broader representation and recognition, the sport is likely to become more accessible and appealing to a wider range of participants. This push for inclusivity extends to advocating for more categories that cater to different body types and fitness goals, thereby dismantling the one-size-fits-all approach. The increasing visibility of diverse role models in the sport is also instrumental in challenging stereotypes and inspiring a new generation of female bodybuilders.

Competition standards and categories in female bodybuilding are expected to undergo significant changes. As the sport grows in popularity and understanding, there is a growing call for a more nuanced approach to judging criteria that appreciates different body types and styles of muscularity. This could lead to the introduction of new categories or the modification of existing ones, offering athletes more tailored and fair competition platforms. The aim is to celebrate a wider array of physiques and athletic achievements, moving away from narrowly defined ideals.

Scientific research continues to profoundly impact training and nutrition in female bodybuilding. As our understanding of the female body's unique responses to training and diet deepens, customized and effective training regimes and dietary plans are being developed. This research is not only enhancing performance and aesthetic results but is also focusing on long-term health and well-being. Future advancements in sports science and nutrition are expected to further optimize the preparation and recovery processes, making bodybuilding a safer and more sustainable sport for women.

The changing social and cultural landscape is set to significantly influence the perception and popularity of female bodybuilding. As societal norms continue to evolve, the appreciation for strength and muscularity in women is likely to grow, breaking down long-standing barriers and misconceptions. The rise of social media and digital platforms offers unprecedented opportunities for exposure and engagement, allowing female bodybuilders to showcase their journeys and achievements, thus attracting new fans and participants.

Part 2: Training

Understanding Muscle Growth

Muscle growth, or hypertrophy, is a complex process that involves more than just the muscles themselves. It's a comprehensive response involving muscle fibers, connective tissues, and neural adaptations. The human muscle is composed primarily of two types of fibers: Type I (slow-twitch) and Type II (fast-twitch). Type I fibers are more endurance-oriented and are less prone to growth, while Type II fibers, used in powerful bursts of movements like lifting weights, have greater potential for growth (American College of Sports Medicine, 2019). The growth of muscle fibers occurs when these fibers experience microtears during intense physical activity. These microtears, when repaired by the body, lead to an increase in muscle size and strength.

The principle of progressive overload is pivotal in muscle growth. It involves consistently increasing the demands on the musculoskeletal system to continually challenge and grow muscles. "To continue to gain benefits, strength training activities need to be done to the point where it's hard for you to do another repetition without help" (Centers for Disease Control and Prevention, 2020). Progressive overload can be achieved by increasing the weight, changing the number of repetitions, altering the speed at which exercises are performed, or varying the rest periods between sets.

Muscle adaptation is a key aspect of hypertrophy. When muscles are exposed to stress regularly, they adapt and grow stronger and larger. However, if the stress is not varied over time, muscles adapt to this stress and growth plateaus. "Muscle growth occurs when the rate of muscle protein synthesis is greater than the rate of muscle protein breakdown" (Journal of Applied Physiology, 2010). This growth only happens if muscles are continually challenged with new stresses.

Nutrition and rest play crucial roles in muscle growth. Adequate protein intake is essential for muscle repair and growth. "The role of nutrition in muscle health is fundamental and should not be overlooked" (Journal of Nutrition, 2018). Proper rest is equally important, as muscle growth occurs during recovery periods, not during the actual lifting of weights. "Recovery, including adequate sleep and time for muscle repair, is as important as the workout itself" (Journal of Sports Sciences, 2018).

Changing workout routines regularly is essential in stimulating continuous muscle growth. This change can involve altering exercises, modifying intensity, or adjusting the volume of workouts. "Variety in your workout routine not only helps keep you motivated but also challenges your muscles in different ways, leading to greater improvements in muscle mass and strength" (American Council on Exercise, 2017). Such changes prevent adaptation and ensure muscles continue to grow.

In summary, understanding muscle growth involves a multifaceted approach that includes knowledge of muscle anatomy, the principle of progressive overload, the necessity of varied stressors, and the importance of nutrition and rest. Effective bodybuilding is not just about lifting weights; it's a systematic approach that requires continuous adjustment and understanding of the body's response to exercise.

Bodybuilding Techniques

Bodybuilding is about pushing the limits of human physiology, where every weight lifted and every set completed is a calculated step towards muscle hypertrophy. The central objective is to continually challenge the muscles, forcing them to adapt and grow. "Muscle growth occurs due to a physiological response to the stress of resistance training" (American Council on Exercise, 2020). This response is fundamental in understanding how bodybuilding transcends mere physical activity and becomes a meticulously planned exercise regimen.

Progressive overload is a cornerstone of effective bodybuilding. It's about incrementally increasing the demands on the musculoskeletal system. "The principle of progressive overload suggests that the continual increase in the total workload during training sessions stimulates muscle growth and strength" (National Strength and Conditioning Association, 2018). By progressively enhancing the intensity, bodybuilders can avoid plateaus - a state where muscles become accustomed to the stress and cease to grow. Overcoming these plateaus is not just about lifting heavier weights; it's about smartly varying the workout routine to continually surprise and challenge the muscles.

Varying the workout routine is essential for sustained muscle growth. Changing exercises, sets, reps, and even the type of resistance ensures that muscles don't become too efficient at any one task. "Muscle confusion is key. It keeps the body guessing and muscles growing" (Muscle & Fitness, 2019). By altering the stimulus, bodybuilders can maintain a state of constant adaptation, crucial for muscle hypertrophy. This strategy also prevents boredom, keeping the workouts both physically and mentally engaging.

Giant sets are an effective technique in bodybuilding. They involve performing multiple exercises for a single muscle group with minimal rest in between. This technique not only saves time but also significantly increases the intensity of the workout, leading to greater muscle fatigue and subsequently, growth. "Giant sets can shock your muscles into growth" (Men's Health, 2017). They provide a high-intensity workout that is efficient and effective for muscle building.

Super sets are another potent strategy, where exercises are performed for opposing muscle groups with little to no rest between. This method not only enhances the intensity but also allows for a more balanced workout, reducing the risk of developing muscular imbalances. "Super sets enable you to do more work in less time, and they make your workouts more dynamic" (Bodybuilding.com, 2016). This time-efficient approach maximizes muscle engagement and promotes balanced development.

Forced reps are a method where a bodybuilder continues to perform repetitions beyond what they could achieve unassisted. This technique requires the help of a spotter and is used to push muscles beyond their usual capacity. "Forced reps can be used to push your muscles beyond their normal failure point, which can lead to increased muscle size and strength" (Journal of Strength and Conditioning Research, 2019). They are particularly useful for overcoming strength plateaus and enhancing muscular endurance.

Eccentric contractions, or negatives, involve focusing on the lowering phase of the lift. This technique can cause more muscle damage, leading to greater growth during recovery. "Eccentric training is more demanding on the muscles and can lead to greater gains in muscle size and strength" (Journal of Applied Physiology, 2020). This approach requires careful execution to avoid injury due to the increased strain it places on muscles.

The concept of 'Twenty-ones' involves breaking a set into three parts to target different ranges of motion within a single exercise. This method increases time under tension, a crucial factor in muscle growth. "Twenty-ones are effective because they prolong the muscle's time under tension" (Muscle & Performance, 2018). This extended tension stimulates the muscles differently compared to traditional sets, aiding in breaking through growth plateaus.

Timed sets involve performing exercises for a fixed duration, focusing on both the concentric and eccentric phases of the movement. "Timing your sets ensures that you maintain tension on the muscles for a set period, which can lead to increased muscle growth" (Journal of Human Kinetics, 2017). This approach emphasizes controlled movements rather than the amount of weight lifted, offering a different stimulus for muscle growth.

Partial reps focus on performing movements within a limited range of motion, either at the start, middle, or end of the movement. This technique allows for targeted muscle stress, especially useful for addressing weak points in a lift. "Partial reps can help overcome sticking points and increase strength in specific ranges of motion" (Strength and Conditioning Journal, 2019). This focused approach can lead to improved overall strength and muscle development.

Pre-exhaustion involves fatiguing a muscle group with an isolation exercise before engaging it in a compound movement. This technique ensures that the targeted muscle reaches fatigue during the compound exercise, leading to enhanced growth. "Pre-exhaustion is effective in ensuring that a specific muscle is thoroughly worked during a compound exercise" (International Journal of Sports Science, 2021). This approach is particularly useful for muscles that are difficult to isolate in compound movements.

Post-exhaustion sets combine heavy and light phases in a single set. This method provides both strength and endurance challenges to the muscles, promoting comprehensive development. "Combining heavy and light loads in a post-exhaustion set can stimulate both myofibrillar and sarcoplasmic hypertrophy" (Journal of Strength and Conditioning Research, 2018). This combination approach can be particularly effective in enhancing overall muscle size and density.

Pyramiding is a technique where the weight, repetitions, or rest periods vary over the course of the sets. This method allows for a gradual increase or decrease in intensity, challenging the muscles in different ways throughout the workout. "Pyramiding allows for a progressive increase in intensity, which can lead to greater muscle growth over time" (National Academy of Sports Medicine, 2019). This strategy is useful for both warming up and cooling down, as well as for intensifying the main workout.

Incorporating these techniques into a bodybuilding regimen can effectively break the monotony and stimulate continuous muscle growth. However, it's vital to understand and respect the body's limits. "Overtraining can lead to injury and setbacks. Listening to your body is crucial" (International Journal of Sports Medicine, 2020). It's essential to balance intensity with adequate rest and recovery to ensure sustainable muscle growth and overall health.

Bodybuilding is not just about lifting weights; it's about lifting smarter, not necessarily heavier. It's a disciplined approach to physical development where strategy is as important as strength. The right combination of techniques can lead to significant improvements in muscle size, strength, and overall physique. Remember, effective bodybuilding is as much about the mind as it is about the body.

Giant Sets

Giant sets are a high-intensity bodybuilding technique, designed to push muscle groups to the brink with minimal rest. This method involves performing three or more exercises consecutively for the same muscle group without taking a break. "Giant sets, by bombarding a muscle with varied stimuli, create an intense muscle-building environment" (Muscle & Fitness, 2021). The goal is to overload the muscle, maximize blood flow, and create a significant 'pump,' leading to increased muscle endurance and size. The effectiveness of giant sets lies in their ability to keep the muscles under constant tension for an extended period, which is a key driver of hypertrophy.

This approach requires meticulous planning, as selecting the right exercises is crucial for maximizing the benefits of giant sets. The exercises chosen should target different angles and aspects of the muscle group to ensure comprehensive development. "By utilizing multiple exercises that target various parts of a muscle, you can achieve more complete muscular development" (Journal of Strength and Conditioning

Research, 2019). The sequence of exercises also matters – starting with the most demanding compound movements and ending with isolation exercises can optimize performance and muscle growth.

The intensity of giant sets makes them especially effective for overcoming plateaus. When traditional workouts fail to yield progress, the shock and stress induced by giant sets can reignite muscle growth. "Giant sets can be particularly effective when you hit a plateau in your training" (Bodybuilding.com, 2020). However, due to their demanding nature, giant sets should be used sparingly to avoid overtraining and ensure adequate recovery.

Recovery is a vital aspect when incorporating giant sets into a workout regimen. The significant stress placed on the muscles requires a focused approach to nutrition and rest. "Post-workout recovery is essential, especially after high-intensity training like giant sets" (International Journal of Sports Nutrition and Exercise Metabolism, 2020). Proper protein intake and rest are crucial for repairing and building the muscles worked during these intense sessions.

In practice, giant sets are not for the faint of heart. They demand a high level of endurance and mental toughness. The ability to push through the burn and fatigue is as much a mental challenge as it is physical. "Mental fortitude plays a significant role in completing giant sets effectively" (Men's Health, 2021). This mental aspect is often what separates those who benefit from this technique and those who find it overwhelming.

Giant sets are not recommended for beginners. They are better suited for intermediate to advanced bodybuilders who have built a solid foundation of strength and endurance. "Giant sets are most effective for those who have already established a baseline of muscle strength and endurance" (Journal of Exercise Science & Fitness, 2021). For those who are ready, however, giant sets can be a game-changer in their muscle-building routine.

Super Sets

Super sets are a dynamic and time-efficient bodybuilding technique where exercises are alternated between opposing muscle groups with minimal to no rest in between. This approach not only enhances the intensity of the workout but also provides a balanced challenge to the body, fostering symmetrical muscle development and reducing the risk of overtraining a specific muscle group. "Super sets are effective in increasing workout intensity and cutting down gym time while balancing the stress on different muscle groups" (Bodybuilding.com, 2018). By immediately switching between exercises, super sets maintain a high heart rate, contributing to improved cardiovascular fitness and increased caloric burn, which is beneficial for those looking to enhance muscle definition alongside size.

The strategic pairing of muscle groups is crucial in super setting. Common pairings include biceps and triceps, chest and back, or quadriceps and hamstrings. These combinations allow one muscle group to rest while the other is working, maximizing workout efficiency. "Strategic muscle pairing in super sets enables continuous workout flow and helps in better muscle recovery" (Journal of Strength and Conditioning Research, 2019). This strategy not only keeps the workout momentum going but also helps in reducing overall workout time, making it a favorite among those with limited time to spend in the gym.

An added advantage of super sets is their ability to increase muscular endurance and stamina. By constantly switching between muscle groups without significant rest, the muscles are trained to recover more quickly, enhancing overall muscular endurance. "Super sets can significantly improve muscular endurance, as they challenge the muscles to perform continuously under stress" (Men's Health, 2020). This endurance is crucial for athletes and bodybuilders alike, as it allows them to sustain longer, more intense training sessions.

However, the intensity of super sets demands a careful approach to avoid overexertion. Proper technique and weight selection are essential to prevent injury. Overloading muscles too quickly or using poor form can lead to strains or other injuries. "While super sets can increase workout intensity, they should be approached with caution, focusing on proper form and appropriate weight selection to avoid injury" (Journal of Exercise Science & Fitness, 2018). It's important for individuals to listen to their bodies and adjust the weights and intensity accordingly.

In conclusion, super sets are a versatile and effective technique for those looking to enhance their workout efficiency, balance muscle development, and improve endurance. Their adaptability to different fitness goals and time constraints makes them a valuable tool in any bodybuilder or athlete's training arsenal. However, like any high-intensity workout technique, they require a mindful approach to execution and progression.

Forced Reps

Forced reps, a technique where a lifter goes beyond muscle failure with the assistance of a partner, significantly intensifies a workout. This method involves performing additional repetitions after reaching the point of muscle fatigue where no more reps could be completed independently. "Forced reps are an effective way to push the muscles beyond their normal fatigue limit, which can stimulate additional muscle growth and strength gains" (Journal of Strength and Conditioning Research, 2018). By extending the set past what one could achieve alone, forced reps create a deeper level of muscle exhaustion and thus, potentially greater muscle hypertrophy.

The key to successful forced reps lies in the careful balance between assistance and effort. The partner's role is to help just enough to keep the weight moving through the sticking point, without taking too much of the load away. "The spotter should assist only to the degree necessary to keep the weight moving, ensuring that the lifter is still exerting maximal effort" (Muscle & Fitness, 2019). This delicate balance ensures that the muscles are still working hard, which is essential for the effectiveness of the forced reps technique.

Incorporating forced reps into a workout regimen should be done judiciously, as the excessive strain can increase the risk of overtraining and injury. This technique is best reserved for experienced lifters who have developed a solid foundation of strength and muscle endurance. "Forced reps should be used sparingly, as they can quickly lead to overtraining if overused" (Bodybuilding.com, 2017). Moreover, they should be applied to only one or two sets per workout, typically at the end of the last set of an exercise.

Proper execution of forced reps requires not only physical effort but also a high level of trust and communication between the lifter and the spotter. The spotter must be attentive and responsive to the lifter's needs, providing the right amount of assistance at the right time. "Effective communication between the lifter and spotter is crucial for the safe and effective execution of forced reps" (Men's Health, 2020). This collaboration is vital to maximize the benefits of the forced reps while minimizing the risk of injury.

Forced reps are a potent tool for muscle growth, offering an advanced method to intensify training and break through strength plateaus. Their effectiveness is grounded in the principle of pushing muscles beyond their usual limits, which can lead to enhanced muscle size and strength. However, their high intensity necessitates a cautious approach, emphasizing proper technique, moderation, and collaboration between the lifter and the spotter.

Eccentric Contractions (Negatives)

Eccentric contractions, often referred to as negatives, are a critical aspect of strength training, emphasizing the muscle lengthening phase of an exercise. These contractions occur when a muscle elongates under tension, usually during the lowering phase of a lift, such as when lowering a dumbbell in a bicep curl. "Eccentric contractions are effective in increasing both muscle strength and size, as they can generate more force compared to concentric contractions" (Journal of Applied Physiology, 2019). This greater force production leads to more significant microtrauma in muscle fibers, which, when repaired, results in muscle growth.

Negatives are known for their intensity and effectiveness in overcoming strength plateaus. Incorporating them into a workout routine can lead to substantial gains in muscle strength and hypertrophy. However, the high level of stress they place on muscles and connective tissues also increases the risk of injury. "While eccentric training is highly effective, it also poses a greater risk of muscle strains and injuries due to the high loads involved" (British Journal of Sports Medicine, 2020). This risk necessitates a careful and progressive approach to incorporating negatives into a training program, especially for those new to this type of exercise.

One of the challenges with eccentric contractions is ensuring proper form and control. The temptation to let gravity do the work is high, but the true benefit of negatives comes from resisting the downward movement in a controlled manner. "Controlled eccentric contractions, where the muscle lengthens slowly and under tension, are crucial for maximizing the benefits of this type of training" (Strength and Conditioning Journal, 2018). This controlled lengthening is what causes the extensive muscle fiber damage, leading to growth during recovery.

Recovery is particularly important with eccentric training due to the increased muscle damage it causes. Ensuring adequate rest and nutrition following workouts that include negatives is essential for allowing the muscles to repair and grow. "Recovery strategies, including proper nutrition and rest, are essential following workouts that include a high volume of eccentric contractions" (International Journal of Sports

Nutrition and Exercise Metabolism, 2019). Neglecting recovery can not only hamper muscle growth but also increase the risk of overtraining and injury.

In conclusion, eccentric contractions or negatives are a powerful tool in the arsenal of strength training techniques. They offer a unique stimulus for muscle growth and strength gains, setting them apart from other types of muscle contractions. However, their intensity and the heightened risk of injury they carry require a thoughtful approach, emphasizing proper technique, gradual progression, and adequate recovery.

Twenty-Ones

Twenty-Ones, a unique bodybuilding technique, divides a single exercise set into three distinct motion ranges, each consisting of seven repetitions, totaling twenty-one reps per set. This method effectively targets a muscle group by varying the range of motion, thereby stimulating muscle fibers differently than traditional sets. "By breaking down a set into three ranges of motion, Twenty-Ones ensure that muscles are under tension throughout the entire range, leading to increased muscle stimulation and growth" (Journal of Strength and Conditioning Research, 2019). The technique typically involves the first seven reps covering the initial half of the movement, the next seven reps covering the final half, and the final seven reps spanning the full range of the exercise.

This approach is particularly effective for exercises like bicep curls or leg extensions, where muscle engagement can vary significantly throughout the movement. The varied range of motion ensures that the muscle is worked thoroughly, reducing the likelihood of strength imbalances. "Twenty-Ones can help target muscles more completely than standard sets, as each part of the muscle range is equally worked" (Men's Health, 2021). This comprehensive muscle engagement is key to developing both muscle strength and size.

One of the main benefits of Twenty-Ones is their impact on muscle endurance and hypertrophy. The high-rep nature of the exercise combined with the varied range of motion creates a significant metabolic stress on the muscles, which is a crucial factor in muscle growth. "The high-rep, varied-range approach of Twenty-Ones significantly enhances metabolic stress on muscles, a key factor in promoting muscle hypertrophy" (Muscle & Fitness, 2020). This metabolic stress leads to an increase in muscle size and endurance over time.

However, due to their intensity, Twenty-Ones should be used judiciously within a workout regimen. Overuse of this technique can lead to excessive muscle fatigue and potential overtraining. It's recommended to incorporate Twenty-Ones sparingly, perhaps as a finishing move in a workout session. "While Twenty-Ones are highly effective, they should be used sparingly to avoid excessive muscle fatigue" (Bodybuilding.com, 2018). This careful integration ensures that the muscles are challenged without being overwhelmed.

In summary, Twenty-Ones offer a unique and effective way to stimulate muscle growth through varied range of motion exercises. By dividing a set into three distinct parts, this technique ensures comprehensive muscle engagement, leading to improved muscle endurance and hypertrophy. The key to their effectiveness lies in the combination of high-rep stress and the targeting of different muscle fibers throughout the range of motion. However, like any intensive exercise technique, they must be integrated thoughtfully into a workout program to maximize benefits while minimizing the risk of overtraining.

Timed Sets/Reps

Timed sets/reps, a method where each repetition is performed over a specific duration, emphasize control and timing in muscle development. This approach diverges from traditional lifting by focusing not on the amount of weight lifted but on the time the muscles spend under tension. "Performing movements over a fixed duration places a different kind of stress on muscles, which can lead to increased muscle development" (Journal of Applied Physiology, 2019). The technique usually involves a slow, controlled movement during both the concentric (lifting) and eccentric (lowering) phases, typically spanning a set time like five seconds up and five seconds down.

This method's effectiveness lies in its ability to maintain constant tension on the muscle, a critical factor for muscle growth. By slowing down the movements, muscles spend more time under load, which can increase muscle fiber recruitment and metabolic stress, leading to growth. "Longer time under tension during timed sets can enhance muscle fiber recruitment, a key factor for muscle hypertrophy" (Journal of Strength and Conditioning Research, 2018). This increased time under tension makes timed sets/reps particularly useful for those looking to improve muscle endurance and achieve hypertrophy.

However, the intensity and demand of timed sets/reps necessitate careful weight selection. Using too heavy a weight can lead to form breakdown, while too light a weight might not provide sufficient stimulus for growth. "Selecting the appropriate weight is crucial in timed sets to ensure the muscles are adequately challenged without compromising form" (Strength and Conditioning Journal, 2020). This balance is vital for maximizing the benefits of the technique while minimizing the risk of injury.

Timed sets/reps also require a significant amount of mental focus and discipline. Maintaining a consistent pace throughout a set demands concentration and resilience, especially as muscle fatigue sets in. "Mental focus and discipline are as important as physical strength in timed sets, as maintaining a consistent pace is challenging" (Muscle & Fitness, 2021). This mental aspect is often what makes timed sets/reps both challenging and rewarding.

In conclusion, timed sets/reps offer a unique approach to muscle development, focusing on controlled movements and the timing of muscle contractions. By emphasizing time under tension rather than the amount of weight lifted, this technique provides a novel stimulus for muscle growth, particularly useful for improving muscle endurance and achieving muscle hypertrophy. However, its effectiveness hinges on appropriate weight selection and mental discipline to maintain a consistent pace throughout the exercise.

Partial Reps

Partial reps, a strength training technique, focus on performing movements within a limited range of motion, often used to overcome strength plateaus or target specific muscle areas. This method involves repeating an exercise movement, but only through a partial range of motion rather than the full extent. "Partial reps are effective for targeting specific muscle groups and can help overcome plateaus in strength training by focusing on the strongest part of the lift" (Journal of Strength and Conditioning Research, 2018). By isolating a portion of the movement, partial reps can intensify the stress and focus on the muscle, leading to increased muscle activation and growth in that specific area.

This technique is particularly beneficial when used at the point of an exercise where the muscle is strongest. For example, in the bench press, lifting the barbell only the top half of the range can target and strengthen the triceps and shoulders. "Utilizing partial reps at the strongest range of a movement can lead to greater strength and muscle gains in that specific area" (Muscle & Fitness, 2019). This focused approach can lead to significant improvements in overall lift strength and performance.

However, the effectiveness of partial reps depends on correct implementation and should not replace full-range exercises entirely. They are best used in conjunction with full-range movements for a well-rounded strength training program. "While partial reps can provide specific muscle benefits, they should be used as a supplement to full-range movements for balanced muscular development" (Men's Health, 2020). This balanced approach ensures comprehensive muscle growth and development.

The risk of overuse injuries should be considered when incorporating partial reps into a workout regimen. Due to the high intensity and stress placed on a specific muscle area, there is an increased risk of strain or injury. "Care should be taken when incorporating partial reps into a workout routine, as the focused intensity on a specific muscle area can lead to a higher risk of overuse injuries" (Bodybuilding.com, 2017). Proper form, weight selection, and adequate recovery are essential to minimize this risk.

In summary, partial reps offer a focused method of stimulating muscle growth and overcoming strength plateaus by isolating specific portions of an exercise's range of motion. They are particularly effective for targeting and strengthening specific muscle areas. However, for balanced muscular development and to avoid the risk of overuse injuries, partial reps should be used in moderation and in conjunction with full-range exercises.

Pre-Exhaustion

Pre-exhaustion is a technique in bodybuilding where an isolation exercise is performed before a compound movement to fatigue a targeted muscle group. This approach ensures that the specific muscle reaches a higher level of fatigue during the subsequent compound exercise. "Pre-exhaustion is used to better target a specific muscle group during compound exercises by fatiguing it with an isolation exercise first" (Journal of Strength and Conditioning Research, 2018). For instance, doing leg extensions to fatigue the quadriceps before performing squats ensures that the quads are thoroughly worked during the squat, even if other muscles involved in the squat are not as fatigued.

This technique is particularly useful when trying to overcome muscle imbalances or to further stimulate muscle growth in a specific area. By pre-exhausting a muscle, bodybuilders can ensure that the targeted muscle group reaches failure during the compound exercise, irrespective of the other, fresher muscles involved. "Pre-exhaustion allows for greater muscle fiber activation of a specific muscle group during compound lifts" (Muscle & Fitness, 2019). It's a strategic way to intensify the workout for a particular muscle, leading to potentially greater gains in size and strength for that muscle group.

However, the technique must be used carefully to avoid excessive fatigue, which could lead to a decrease in performance during the compound exercises or increase the risk of injury. The key is to fatigue the muscle, not to annihilate it before the compound movement. "The goal of pre-exhaustion is to fatigue the muscle, not to completely deplete it before the main compound exercise" (Men's Health, 2020). This approach ensures that the muscle is adequately challenged without compromising the overall workout quality or increasing the risk of injury.

Incorporating pre-exhaustion into a training program requires careful planning and attention to the body's response. It is not suitable for every workout and should be used selectively based on training goals and the body's recovery ability. "Selective use of pre-exhaustion, based on training goals and recovery, is crucial for its effectiveness" (Bodybuilding.com, 2018). Listening to the body and adjusting the intensity of the pre-exhaustion and the subsequent compound exercises is essential for maximizing the benefits of this technique.

Post-Exhaustion Sets

Post-exhaustion sets combine the use of heavy and light weights within a single exercise sequence to intensively train muscle groups. This method typically involves performing a set with heavy weights for fewer repetitions, immediately followed by a set with lighter weights for higher repetitions. "Post-exhaustion sets are effective in stimulating both types of muscle hypertrophy - myofibrillar through heavy sets and sarcoplasmic through lighter, higher-rep sets" (Journal of Strength and Conditioning Research, 2018). This combination allows bodybuilders to target both strength and muscle size within the same exercise, making it a time-efficient and comprehensive muscle-building technique.

The effectiveness of post-exhaustion sets lies in their ability to exhaust the muscle through different stimulus types. The heavy sets focus on maximal strength and muscle fiber recruitment, while the lighter sets target muscular endurance and metabolic stress. "By combining heavy and light sets, post-exhaustion training effectively fatigues the muscle through different pathways, potentially leading to greater overall muscle growth" (Men's Health, 2019). This dual approach ensures that muscles are thoroughly worked, enhancing growth and strength gains.

However, the intensity of post-exhaustion sets requires careful attention to muscle recovery and overall training volume. Due to the significant stress placed on muscles, ensuring adequate rest and nutrition is crucial for recovery and growth. "Adequate recovery strategies are essential when employing post-exhaustion sets due to the high level of muscle stress involved" (International Journal of Sports Nutrition and Exercise Metabolism, 2020). Overuse of this technique without proper recovery can lead to overtraining and hinder muscle growth.

Implementing post-exhaustion sets into a workout regimen should be done with consideration of one's overall training plan and goals. It's a technique well-suited for intermediate to advanced bodybuilders looking to intensify their workouts and challenge their muscles in new ways.

"Post-exhaustion sets are most effective when strategically implemented into a well-rounded training program, especially for those seeking to overcome plateaus in muscle growth" (Bodybuilding.com, 2018). This careful integration ensures maximum benefit while minimizing the risk of injury or overtraining.

Pyramiding

Pyramiding is a versatile bodybuilding technique involving progressive adjustments in weight (load), repetitions, or rest intervals within consecutive sets of an exercise. In load pyramiding, weight increases with each set while the number of repetitions typically decreases, intensifying the challenge for the muscles. "Load pyramiding allows for a gradual increase in weight, effectively warming up the muscles in the initial sets and maximizing strength in the latter sets" (Journal of Strength and Conditioning Research, 2019). This method is particularly effective for building strength, as it allows for heavy lifting when the muscles are thoroughly warmed up.

Repetition pyramiding, on the other hand, involves altering the number of repetitions per set, either increasing or decreasing across the sets. This can either start with high reps and low weight, gradually moving to low reps and high weight, or vice versa. "Repetition pyramiding challenges the muscles by varying the volume and intensity within a workout, which can lead to increased muscle endurance and hypertrophy" (Men's Health, 2020). This variation in volume and intensity can stimulate muscle growth in different ways compared to a standard set structure.

Rest pyramiding adjusts the rest intervals between sets, usually starting with shorter rest periods and increasing them with each set, or the reverse. This technique manipulates the recovery time of the muscles, impacting the intensity of the workout. "Adjusting rest intervals in a pyramiding manner can significantly influence the intensity and focus of a workout, affecting both strength and endurance" (Muscle & Fitness,

2021). By manipulating rest periods, bodybuilders can target different aspects of muscle performance.

Incorporating pyramiding techniques into a training program requires careful planning and an understanding of one's training goals. Whether focusing on load, repetitions, or rest, each method of pyramiding offers a unique way to challenge the muscles, leading to different training adaptations. "Strategic use of different pyramiding techniques can optimize a training program to meet specific strength, size, or endurance goals" (Bodybuilding.com, 2018). This customization is what makes pyramiding a popular and effective approach in strength training and bodybuilding.

Advanced Training Techniques

Load Pyramiding and Load Sets

Load pyramiding and load sets are key techniques in advanced strength training, focusing on progressively increasing the weight while varying the number of repetitions. Load pyramiding typically involves starting with lighter weights and higher repetitions, gradually increasing the weight and decreasing the repetitions across successive sets. This method not only warms up the muscles effectively but also prepares them for the heavier loads to come, maximizing strength and hypertrophy gains. "Load pyramiding is an effective way to progressively overload the muscles, leading to significant increases in strength and muscle size" (Journal of Strength and Conditioning Research, 2019). Load sets, on the other hand, involve increasing the weight within a single set, often immediately after a set number of repetitions. This approach intensifies the stress on the muscles within the same set, challenging them further and promoting muscle growth. "Incorporating load sets within a workout can significantly increase muscle stimulation, as it combines volume and intensity in a single set" (Strength and Conditioning

Journal, 2020). Both techniques are designed to push the muscles beyond their comfort zone, promoting adaptation and growth.

Break-downs

Break-downs are an advanced bodybuilding technique designed to intensify workouts by reducing weights immediately after reaching muscle failure. This method involves performing an exercise until no more repetitions are possible, then quickly lowering the weight and continuing to do more repetitions until failure is reached again. "Break downs extend a set past the point of initial muscle failure, allowing for deeper muscle fiber recruitment and enhanced muscle fatigue, which are key drivers for muscle hypertrophy" (Journal of Strength and Conditioning Research, 2020). By pushing the muscles beyond their usual limits, break downs create a highly intense environment that can lead to increased muscle growth and endurance. This technique is particularly effective for experienced lifters seeking to overcome plateaus and enhance their muscle gains. However, due to its intensity, break downs should be used cautiously to avoid overtraining and ensure adequate muscle recovery.

Pre-exhaustion with Break-downs

Combining pre-exhaustion with break-downs is an advanced bodybuilding strategy that maximizes muscle growth by integrating two intense techniques. Pre-exhaustion involves performing an isolation exercise to target a specific muscle group before a compound movement, ensuring the targeted muscle reaches fatigue early in the compound exercise. "Pre-exhaustion effectively fatigues a muscle group before a compound exercise, ensuring it is fully activated throughout the workout" (Journal of Strength and Conditioning Research, 2019). Break-downs, performed after reaching muscle failure, involve immediately reducing the weight and continuing with more repetitions. This combination is powerful: pre-exhaustion ensures the muscle group is already fatigued when starting the compound exercise, and break-downs push these muscles beyond their normal failure point. "The combination of pre-exhaustion and break-downs can lead to heightened muscle activation and superior hypertrophy, compared to using these techniques in isolation" (Strength and Conditioning Journal, 2021). This approach requires careful monitoring to avoid overtraining and ensure adequate recovery, given its high intensity.

Workout Schedules and Routines

Creating an effective workout schedule is essential for optimal muscle development and overall fitness. A well-planned routine targets different muscle groups on specific days, allowing for focused training and adequate recovery time. For instance, a common weekly layout might designate Monday for chest exercises, such as bench presses and push-ups, ensuring a powerful start to the week. Tuesday could then shift focus to back muscles with exercises like rows and lat pull-downs, allowing the chest muscles to recover while engaging a different set of muscles. Midweek, attention could turn to the lower body, with Wednesday dedicated to leg workouts, including squats, lunges, and leg presses, providing a comprehensive lower body routine.

Continuing through the week, Thursday might focus on shoulders, incorporating movements like overhead presses and lateral raises to target all aspects of the deltoids. On Friday, the routine could shift to arms, with bicep curls and tricep extensions, ensuring these smaller muscle groups receive dedicated attention. The weekend can then offer a change of pace: Saturday might include a lighter, full-body workout or cardio session, promoting active recovery and cardiovascular health, while Sunday could be reserved for complete rest or light activities like walking or yoga, allowing the body to recover and prepare for the upcoming week.

This schedule is just a template and should be adjusted based on individual needs and goals. For someone focusing on building size and strength, incorporating heavy weights with lower repetitions would be key, while someone aiming for endurance and toning might focus on higher repetitions with lighter weights. Each workout session should last around 45 to 60 minutes, striking a balance between intensity and overtraining.

In addition to this weekly structure, it's vital to periodically change the routine. Varying exercises, order, intensity, and volume can prevent plateaus, a state where the body adapts to the workout, slowing progress. "Muscle confusion, or changing your workout routine regularly, can help maximize muscle growth and prevent plateaus" (Bodybuilding.com, 2021). This variation can be as simple as substituting barbells for dumbbells, altering the grip or angle of an exercise, or incorporating completely new exercises.

The intensity of each workout should be balanced with adequate rest and nutrition. Each muscle group needs time to recover and grow after being exercised, typically requiring 48 to 72 hours. Hence, organizing the workout schedule to avoid training the same muscle group on consecutive days is crucial. "Giving each muscle group adequate time to recover is as important as the workout itself for muscle growth" (Journal of Exercise Science & Fitness, 2020). Adequate protein intake and hydration, alongside quality sleep, are also integral to support muscle recovery and growth.

Tailoring the routine to personal goals, experience level, and physical condition is essential. Beginners might start with lighter weights and basic compound movements, gradually increasing intensity as their strength and endurance improve. More experienced lifters might incorporate advanced techniques like supersets, dropsets, or pyramiding to further challenge their muscles. "Personalizing your workout routine is key to achieving your fitness goals and prevents the risk of injury" (Men's Health, 2021). This personalization ensures the workout remains challenging yet achievable, minimizing the risk of injury and maximizing the potential for muscle growth and fitness improvements.

Overall, the key to a successful workout schedule is balance – balancing different muscle groups, balancing intensity with rest, and balancing personal goals with effective training strategies. A well-planned workout schedule, when combined with proper nutrition and rest, can lead to significant improvements in muscle size, strength, and overall fitness.

Personalizing Your Workout

Personalizing your workout is crucial for effectiveness and safety, catering to individual fitness levels, goals, and body responses. For beginners, it's essential to start with basic exercises that build foundational strength and endurance. Starting with lighter weights and focusing on form can prevent injuries and build a solid base. "Beginners should focus on mastering form with lighter weights before progressing to heavier loads" (American Council on Exercise, 2020). Initially, full-body workouts two to three times a week can help acclimate the body to strength training. As strength and comfort with the exercises increase, the workout can be gradually intensified by increasing weights, adding more sets, or incorporating more challenging exercises.

For intermediate lifters, the focus shifts to more specialized routines that target specific muscle groups. This can involve splitting workouts into upper and lower body days, or isolating specific muscle groups each day. Intermediate lifters can start experimenting with different types of equipment and techniques, such as dumbbells, barbells, and resistance machines. "Intermediate lifters should begin to incorporate a variety of equipment and techniques to challenge their muscles in different ways" (Journal of Strength and Conditioning Research, 2019). This is also a stage where lifters can start to introduce techniques like supersets or drop sets to intensify their workouts.

Advanced bodybuilders require a more strategic approach, often focusing on very specific muscle development and strength goals. Their routines might involve a high degree of specialization with advanced techniques like pyramiding, pre-exhaustion, and periodization. "Advanced bodybuilders should employ a range of specialized techniques to continue challenging their muscles and avoid plateaus" (Muscle & Fitness, 2021). Advanced lifters also need to be particularly mindful of their body's response to training, carefully balancing intensity, volume, and recovery to optimize growth and prevent injury.

Regardless of the level, rest and recovery are vital components of any training regimen. Muscles need time to repair and grow after a workout. Overtraining can lead to fatigue, decreased performance, and increased risk of injury. "Adequate rest and recovery are as important as the workout itself, allowing for muscle repair and growth" (Journal of Sports Sciences, 2018). This includes not only rest days but also ensuring adequate sleep and proper nutrition, particularly sufficient protein intake for muscle repair.

Incorporating variety in workouts is important to keep the body guessing and muscles adapting. Changing up the routine every few weeks can prevent boredom and plateauing. This could mean altering the exercises, adjusting the number of repetitions and sets, or changing the order of the workout. "Regularly changing your workout routine is essential for continuous improvement and to keep the workouts engaging" (Bodybuilding.com, 2020).

Personalizing a workout also means listening to your body and adjusting the workout accordingly. This might involve reducing intensity if feeling fatigued or stepping up the workout if it feels too easy. Being in tune with your body helps in customizing the workout to meet individual needs effectively. "Listening to your body and adjusting your workout accordingly is key for effective and safe training" (Men's Health, 2021).

Workout Splits Introduction

Workout splits are systematic approaches to dividing physical training across different days, focusing on specific muscle groups or types of exercise in each session. This methodical separation allows for targeted muscle engagement and recovery, a critical aspect in building strength, endurance, and overall fitness. Understanding workout splits is crucial for anyone serious about their fitness routine, whether a beginner or an experienced athlete. The right split can significantly enhance training results by optimizing muscle recovery, preventing overtraining, and ensuring a balanced workout regimen.

The first step in understanding workout splits is recognizing their fundamental purpose: to allocate specific days to work on different muscle groups or fitness aspects. For instance, a typical split might designate separate days for upper body, lower body, and cardiovascular training. This separation is not a mere whim of fitness enthusiasts but is rooted in the science of muscle recovery and growth. When a muscle group is intensely worked out, it needs time to repair and strengthen. Without adequate rest, muscles cannot recover fully, leading to a plateau or even a decline in performance and an increased risk of injury. Workout splits respect this physiological need by providing rest periods for each muscle group while allowing other parts of the body to be trained.

Another critical aspect of workout splits is their adaptability. They can be tailored to individual needs, goals, and schedules. For instance, a three-day split might work for someone with limited time, focusing on full-body workouts each session. In contrast, a five or six-day split could allow more dedicated focus on each muscle group, ideal for those aiming for hypertrophy or specialized athletic training. The flexibility of workout splits means they can be adjusted as goals or circumstances change, making them a sustainable approach to fitness.

Selecting the right workout split requires an understanding of one's own goals and physical condition. A beginner might benefit from a full-body workout split, where each session involves exercises targeting all major muscle groups. This approach promotes overall muscular balance and strength, a foundation upon which more specialized training can be built. On the other hand, someone with specific goals, like building muscle mass or improving athletic performance, might opt for a split that allows for more focused and intense training on specific muscle groups.

Experience level plays a significant role in choosing a workout split. Beginners often respond well to full-body routines as their bodies are not yet accustomed to high-intensity or high-volume training. As one progresses, the body adapts and may require more targeted stimuli for further improvement. This adaptation is where more advanced splits, such as upper/lower or push/pull/legs, come into play. These splits allow for more intense sessions with a higher volume of exercises for each muscle group, necessitating a longer recovery period for each.

While workout splits are predominantly about training, they cannot be separated from the context of overall fitness, which includes nutrition, rest, and lifestyle factors. Proper nutrition provides the energy and building blocks needed for exercise and recovery. A diet lacking in essential nutrients or energy can undermine the effectiveness of even the most well-planned workout split. Similarly, rest and sleep are not just times of inactivity but critical periods when the body repairs and strengthens itself. Neglecting rest can lead to overtraining, fatigue, and a decrease in performance.

It's also essential to be aware of the common mistakes people make with workout splits. One of the most frequent errors is not allowing adequate recovery time, leading to overtraining and potential injuries. Another mistake is focusing too much on preferred exercises or muscle groups, leading to imbalances and weaknesses. A well-designed workout split should provide a balanced approach to training, ensuring that all major muscle groups are worked and developed evenly.

Periodic assessment and adjustment of workout splits are necessary. As the body adapts to a specific training routine, it may require new challenges to continue progressing. This adaptation is why it's advisable to periodically review and modify workout routines. Adjustments can include changing the exercises, increasing the intensity or volume of workouts, or even switching to a different type of split altogether.

In conclusion, workout splits are powerful tools in the arsenal of fitness training. They offer a structured approach to exercise, ensuring balanced training, adequate recovery, and continual progression. Whether you are just starting your fitness journey or looking to optimize your training, understanding and effectively utilizing workout splits can significantly enhance your results. This chapter has provided the foundational knowledge needed to comprehend and apply these principles, empowering you to take control of your fitness regimen with confidence and clarity.

The Essence of Workout Splits

Workout splits represent a strategic division of exercise routines, crucial for achieving specific fitness goals. They are not mere scheduling conveniences but a deliberate method to enhance training effectiveness and efficiency. At their core, workout splits involve dividing exercise routines across different days to focus on specific muscle groups or types of exercise each session. This methodical approach allows for targeted muscle engagement and adequate recovery, vital in building strength, endurance, and overall fitness. Understanding workout splits is essential for anyone serious about their fitness regimen, whether they are a novice or an experienced athlete.

The primary purpose of workout splits is to allocate specific days to work on different muscle groups or fitness aspects. For example, a typical split might designate separate days for upper body, lower body, and cardiovascular training. This separation aligns with the science of muscle recovery and growth. Intense workouts require muscles to repair and strengthen, necessitating time for recovery. Without adequate rest, muscles cannot recover fully, leading to a plateau or decline in performance and an increased risk of injury. Workout splits respect this physiological need by providing rest periods for each muscle group while allowing other parts of the body to be trained.

Adaptability is a key feature of workout splits. They can be tailored to individual needs, goals, and schedules. A three-day split might work for someone with limited time, focusing on full-body workouts each session. In contrast, a five or six-day split could allow more dedicated focus on each muscle group, ideal for those aiming for hypertrophy or specialized athletic training. The flexibility of workout splits means they can be adjusted as goals or circumstances change, making them a sustainable approach to fitness.

Selecting the right workout split requires an understanding of one's own goals and physical condition. A beginner might benefit from a full-body workout split, where each session involves exercises targeting all major muscle groups. This approach promotes overall muscular balance and strength, a foundation upon which more specialized training can be built. Conversely, someone with specific goals, like building muscle mass or improving athletic performance, might opt for a split that allows for more focused and intense training on specific muscle groups.

Experience level plays a significant role in choosing a workout split. Beginners often respond well to full-body routines as their bodies are not yet accustomed to high-intensity or high-volume training. As one progresses, the body adapts and may require more targeted stimuli for further improvement. This adaptation is where more advanced splits, such as upper/lower or push/pull/legs, come into play. These splits allow for more intense sessions with a higher volume of exercises for each muscle group, necessitating a longer recovery period for each.

While workout splits are predominantly about training, they cannot be separated from the context of overall fitness, which includes nutrition, rest, and lifestyle factors. Proper nutrition provides the energy and building blocks needed for exercise and recovery. A diet lacking in essential nutrients or energy can undermine the effectiveness of even the most well-planned workout split. Similarly, rest and sleep are not just times of inactivity but critical periods when the body repairs and strengthens itself. Neglecting rest can lead to overtraining, fatigue, and a decrease in performance.

It's also essential to be aware of the common mistakes people make with workout splits. One of the most frequent errors is not allowing adequate recovery time, leading to overtraining and potential injuries. Another mistake is focusing too much on preferred exercises or muscle groups, leading to imbalances and weaknesses. A well-designed workout split should provide a balanced approach to training, ensuring that all major muscle groups are worked and developed evenly.

Periodic assessment and adjustment of workout splits are necessary. As the body adapts to a specific training routine, it may require new challenges to continue progressing. This adaptation is why it's advisable to periodically review and modify workout routines. Adjustments can include changing the exercises, increasing the intensity or volume of workouts, or even switching to a different type of split altogether.

In conclusion, workout splits are powerful tools in the arsenal of fitness training. They offer a structured approach to exercise, ensuring balanced training, adequate recovery, and continual progression. Whether you are just starting your fitness journey or looking to optimize your training, understanding and effectively utilizing workout splits can significantly enhance your results. This chapter has provided the foundational knowledge needed to comprehend and apply these principles, empowering you to take control of your fitness regimen with confidence and clarity.

The Science Behind Splitting Workouts

Workout splits are integral to effective fitness regimes, allowing for optimized muscle recovery, minimized risk of overtraining, and enhanced muscle growth. The science behind these benefits is rooted in understanding how the human body responds to stress, particularly the stress of exercise. When muscles are subjected to the strain of weight lifting or intense physical activity, they experience microscopic tears. This damage, while sounding negative, is the catalyst for muscle growth and strength increase. During the recovery period, the body repairs these tears, and in doing so, the muscles grow stronger and larger. However, this process requires time and the right conditions, including adequate rest and proper nutrition.

The principle of recovery is where workout splits play a crucial role. By dividing the training schedule into segments that focus on different muscle groups, workout splits allow certain areas of the body to rest and recover while others are being worked. For example, an upper/lower split allows the upper body muscles to rest while the lower body is trained, and vice versa. This approach not only prevents overworking any single muscle group but also ensures that each has the maximum amount of time to recover before being stressed again.

Optimized recovery is essential not just for muscle growth but also for avoiding overtraining syndrome. Overtraining occurs when there's an imbalance between training and recovery, where the body does not have sufficient time to recuperate between workouts. Symptoms of overtraining include prolonged fatigue, decreased performance, and even injury. By utilizing workout splits, the risk of overtraining is significantly reduced as each muscle group is given ample time to recover.

Workout splits also contribute to increased muscle hypertrophy, which is the enlargement of muscle cells. When a muscle group is targeted with sufficient intensity during a workout, it triggers the body's anabolic processes, which repair and build muscle tissue. This process is most efficient when the muscle group is allowed to fully recover before being worked again. Different types of workout splits cater to different training goals and intensities, enabling individuals to tailor their training according to their specific hypertrophy goals.

In addition to muscle recovery and growth, workout splits also aid in better workout planning and execution. By having a structured plan that clearly defines which muscle groups to work on and when it allows for more focused and effective workouts. This structure ensures that all major muscle groups are worked evenly over time, promoting balanced muscular development and reducing the likelihood of muscle imbalances.

Nutrition plays a complementary role in the effectiveness of workout splits. Adequate protein intake is crucial for muscle repair and growth, while carbohydrates provide the energy needed for intense workouts. Ensuring a balanced intake of macronutrients, vitamins, and minerals supports the body's recovery processes and overall health, which in turn maximizes the benefits gained from workout splits.

Flexibility in workout splits is another key factor in their effectiveness. Individuals can adjust the frequency, intensity, and volume of workouts in their split to match their personal fitness level, goals, and schedule. This flexibility allows for progressive overload, where the intensity of workouts is gradually increased to challenge the muscles continuously and promote further growth and strength gains.

Workout splits also have a psychological benefit, providing a clear and structured approach to training that can boost motivation and focus. Knowing exactly what to train on a given day reduces decision fatigue and increases adherence to a fitness regimen. This structured approach also makes it easier to track progress and make adjustments as needed.

Tailoring Your Split: Factors to Consider

When it comes to tailoring a workout split, several key factors must be considered to ensure the regimen is effective, sustainable, and aligned with personal goals. One of the primary considerations is the individual's experience level. Beginners often benefit from simpler workout splits. These typically involve full-body routines or compound movements that engage multiple muscle groups simultaneously. Such routines are not only efficient for those new to exercising but also provide a solid foundation for overall fitness and muscle development. As individuals become more experienced and their bodies adapt to regular training, they may require more specialized splits. Advanced athletes or those with specific strength or bodybuilding goals might opt for splits that isolate muscle groups, allowing for more focused and intense training on each area.

Fitness goals are another critical factor in determining the right workout split. For strength building, splits that allow for heavy lifting with ample recovery time for each muscle group are ideal. These often involve working different muscle groups on different days, such as an upper/lower split or a push/pull/legs split. For endurance enhancement, a mix of cardiovascular training and strength training might be necessary, with more frequent but less intense workouts. Those aiming for fat loss might benefit from a combination of strength training and high-intensity interval training (HIIT) to maximize calorie burn.

Time availability is a practical consideration that significantly influences the choice of workout split. The amount of time one can dedicate to working out each week will determine the feasibility and effectiveness of different splits. Individuals with limited time may opt for full-body workouts that can be done two or three times a week. In contrast, those with more time available might choose a split that allows for daily training, focusing on different muscle groups each day for more detailed muscle sculpting and strength gains.

Individual recovery rates are crucial in dictating the intensity and frequency of workouts. Recovery is when muscles repair and grow stronger, and it varies from person to person. Some individuals may recover quickly and be able to handle high-frequency training, while others might need longer recovery periods to avoid overtraining and injury. Listening to the body and adjusting the workout split accordingly is essential for long-term progress and health.

Finally, equipment access also plays a role in determining the type of exercises included in a workout split. Those with access to a fully equipped gym have a wider range of exercises to choose from, allowing for more variety and specificity in their training. However, individuals working out at home with limited equipment can still achieve effective workouts by focusing on bodyweight exercises, dumbbells, or resistance bands. The key is to choose a split and exercises that align with the available resources while still challenging the body and progressing toward fitness goals.

Tailoring a workout split requires careful consideration of several factors, including experience level, fitness goals, time availability, individual recovery rates, and equipment access. By addressing these factors, individuals can design a workout split that is not only effective in helping them reach their fitness goals but also enjoyable and sustainable in the long run. The right workout split is a powerful tool in any fitness journey, providing structure and direction while accommodating individual needs and circumstances.

A Balanced Approach: Combining Science with Individual Needs

The effectiveness of workout splits hinges on a crucial balance between scientific principles and individual needs. This balance is what makes a workout split not just a regimen, but a personalized fitness plan that aligns with specific goals, preferences, and lifestyle. The foundational aspects of workout splits are rooted in exercise science, focusing on how the body responds to different types of training stimuli. By understanding these principles, one can create a workout split that maximizes muscle growth, strength gains, and overall fitness.

One of the key scientific principles underlying workout splits is the concept of muscle hypertrophy, which involves increasing muscle size through resistance training. To achieve hypertrophy, muscles must be subjected to a level of stress that challenges them beyond their current capacity. This is where the design of workout splits comes into play. By dividing training into sessions that focus on different muscle groups, individuals can apply the necessary stress to each muscle group while allowing others to recover. This approach not only maximizes muscle growth but also minimizes the risk of overtraining and injury.

Another scientific aspect critical to workout splits is the principle of progressive overload. This involves gradually increasing the weight, frequency, or intensity of workouts to continuously challenge the muscles. A well-designed workout split should incorporate this principle, allowing for consistent progress over time. Whether it's adding more weight to the barbell or increasing the number of reps and sets, progressive overload is a fundamental element of successful workout regimens.

While these scientific principles are essential, the effectiveness of a workout split also heavily depends on personal factors. Individual fitness goals play a significant role in shaping the structure of a workout split. For example, someone aiming for general fitness might prefer a full-body workout split that provides a balanced approach to muscle development. In contrast, an individual focused on bodybuilding might opt for a split that isolates specific muscle groups, allowing for more targeted and intense training.

Personal preferences and lifestyle are also crucial in determining the right workout split. Factors like schedule constraints, workout enjoyment, and motivation levels need to be considered. A workout split that aligns with an individual's daily routine and personal preferences is more likely to be sustainable and enjoyable. For instance, someone with a busy schedule might find a three-day full-body workout more manageable than a six-day split.

Recovery capabilities are another personal factor that must be taken into account. Recovery is a critical component of fitness, as muscles grow and repair during rest periods. Individuals need to consider their own recovery rates when designing a workout split. Some may recover quickly and be able to handle frequent and intense workouts, while others may require more rest days to avoid fatigue and overtraining.

Finally, equipment availability can influence the choice of exercises in a workout split. Those with access to a well-equipped gym can incorporate a wide range of exercises in their routine, from machine-based workouts to free weights. However, those working out at home with limited equipment can still have effective workouts by focusing on bodyweight exercises and using whatever equipment they have available.

The Full Body Split

The full body split is a foundational approach to strength training and overall fitness. This regimen entails targeting all major muscle groups within a single workout session, and is typically executed two to three times a week. Such a frequency ensures that each muscle group receives adequate attention while allowing substantial recovery time between sessions. This split is particularly beneficial for muscle growth and overall fitness improvement, making it an excellent choice for both beginners and seasoned athletes.

For beginners, the full body split serves as an introduction to strength training, covering all bases in a few sessions per week. It provides a holistic approach, ensuring that no major muscle group is neglected. This split is beneficial for building a strong foundation of muscle strength and endurance, which is crucial for more advanced training. Moreover, it's an efficient way to exercise, especially for those with limited time, as it offers a comprehensive workout in a single session.

Experienced athletes also find value in the full body split. It can be used as a method of maintaining muscle mass and strength, or as a way to break through plateaus by changing the routine. This split allows for a high degree of flexibility in terms of exercise selection, intensity, and volume. Advanced lifters can incorporate a range of exercises, from compound movements like squats, deadlifts, and bench presses, to isolation exercises targeting specific muscle groups.

One of the key advantages of the full body split is the balanced development it promotes. By engaging all major muscle groups in a single session, it ensures that no part of the body is over or under-trained. This balance is crucial not only for aesthetic purposes but also for functional strength and injury prevention. A well-rounded physique is less prone to injuries and better equipped to handle various physical challenges.

Recovery is another significant aspect of the full body split. Since this routine is typically spread out over two to three days a week, it allows muscles adequate time to recover and grow. Recovery is a critical part of the muscle-building process; without it, muscles cannot repair the micro-tears that occur during strength training. This split provides the perfect balance between training and rest, making it ideal for sustained muscle growth.

The full body split also offers versatility in terms of intensity and volume. Depending on individual fitness goals and preferences, one can adjust the number of exercises, sets, and reps for each muscle group. Beginners might start with fewer exercises and lower volume, gradually increasing as they become more comfortable and their fitness improves. On the other hand, more advanced athletes might focus on increasing the intensity of their workouts, either by adding more weight, incorporating advanced techniques like supersets and drop sets, or reducing rest periods between sets.

Another benefit of the full body split is its effectiveness for fat loss. By engaging multiple large muscle groups in a single session, it creates a high metabolic demand, burning a significant number of calories both during and after the workout. This makes it an efficient tool for those looking to lose weight while maintaining or building muscle mass.

Balanced muscle development is a cornerstone of the full body split. Each session targets every major muscle group, ensuring a harmonious development of the entire body. This holistic approach prevents the common issue of muscle imbalances that can occur with more specialized splits. For instance, focusing excessively on the upper body while neglecting the lower body can lead to disproportion and potentially increase the risk of injuries. The full body split circumvents this by providing a balanced workout routine, promoting symmetrical muscle growth and functional strength.

Flexibility is another significant benefit. The full body split can be easily adapted to various schedules and fitness levels, making it a practical choice for a broad range of individuals. Whether one is a busy professional with limited time for the gym, a stay-at-home parent juggling numerous responsibilities, or someone who travels frequently, this split can be tailored to fit into almost any lifestyle. The workouts can be compressed or extended based on time constraints and personal preferences, making it a highly adaptable training approach.

Efficiency is a key attribute of the full body split, particularly appealing to those with limited time. Each session delivers a complete workout, engaging all major muscle groups. This means that even if an individual can only spare a few days a week for exercise, they can still achieve comprehensive fitness results. This efficiency makes the full body split an excellent choice for people who want to maximize their workout time.

Recovery-friendly nature of the full body split is crucial for muscle repair and growth. Ample rest between sessions is provided, allowing each muscle group to recover fully before being worked again. This rest period is essential for the repair of muscle fibers that break down during exercise, a process that leads to muscle growth and strength gains. Adequate recovery also reduces the risk of overtraining and injuries, making the full body split a sustainable and safe workout regimen.

The variety offered in the full body split keeps workouts engaging and challenging. Unlike routines that repetitively focus on the same muscle groups, the full body split allows for a wide range of exercises targeting different areas of the body. This variety not only prevents boredom but also challenges muscles in diverse ways, contributing to better overall fitness and preventing plateauing.

Sample full body workout routines demonstrate the adaptability of this split to different fitness levels. Beginners can focus on compound movements like squats, bench presses, deadlifts, and overhead presses, interspersed with bodyweight exercises like push-ups and planks. These foundational exercises build overall strength and muscle endurance, providing a solid base for more advanced training.

For intermediate fitness enthusiasts, incorporating more variety in the routine is beneficial. This can include exercises like lunges, pull-ups, and dumbbell rows, which build on the foundation set by the basic compound movements. These exercises introduce new challenges and help continue the development of strength and muscle mass.

Advanced routines can add complexity with plyometric exercises, supersets, and higher intensity training techniques. These additions increase the intensity of the workouts, pushing the limits of strength, endurance, and muscular power. Advanced routines are designed to challenge even the most experienced athletes, ensuring continuous progression and development.

The full body split is ideal for various individuals, each with unique reasons for choosing this approach. Beginners find it beneficial as it offers a foundational approach to strength and fitness, covering all bases in a few sessions per week. This solid foundation is crucial for future progression in more specialized or intense training routines.

Individuals with limited time find the full body split ideal as it allows them to maintain a high level of fitness with just a few gym sessions each week. Every session is comprehensive, ensuring that despite the limited frequency, the effectiveness of their workouts is not compromised.

Those seeking balanced development, aiming for overall fitness rather than specializing in one area, benefit greatly from the full body split. It ensures that all muscle groups receive equal attention, leading to a well-rounded physique and functional strength.

Lastly, recovery-conscious individuals, including those who need or prefer more rest days due to personal preferences, lifestyle constraints, or age, find the full body split aligns well with their requirements. The built-in rest periods between workout days help in maintaining a healthy balance between exercise and recovery, crucial

Example Full Body Workout Routines

Full body workout routines can be tailored to suit various fitness levels, from beginners to advanced trainers. Each level focuses on different types of exercises and intensities to match the individual's skill and strength.

Beginner Routine

For beginners, the focus is on mastering the basic compound movements, which work multiple muscle groups simultaneously, providing a solid foundation for strength and muscle development. A typical beginner's full body routine might include:

- Squats: 3 sets of 8-10 reps. Squats are fundamental for building lower body strength and engaging core muscles.

- Bench Press: 3 sets of 8-10 reps. This exercise targets the chest, shoulders, and triceps.

- Deadlifts: 3 sets of 8-10 reps. Deadlifts are excellent for developing the back, glutes, and hamstrings.

- Overhead Press: 3 sets of 8-10 reps. This movement strengthens the shoulders and upper back.

- Push-Ups: 2 sets of 10-15 reps. Push-ups are a great bodyweight exercise for the chest, triceps, and shoulders.

- Planks: 2 sets, holding for 30 seconds to 1 minute. Planks are effective for core strengthening.

This routine should be performed two to three times a week, with at least one day of rest between sessions to allow for muscle recovery.

Intermediate Routine

Intermediate routines introduce more variety and slightly higher intensity. The addition of new exercises helps to further challenge the muscles and promote continued growth and strength gains.

- Lunges: 3 sets of 10 reps per leg. Lunges are great for targeting the quadriceps, glutes, and hamstrings.

- Pull-Ups: 3 sets of 6-8 reps. Pull-ups are effective for strengthening the upper back, biceps, and forearms.

- Dumbbell Rows: 3 sets of 8-10 reps per arm. This exercise focuses on the back muscles and biceps.

- Incline Bench Press: 3 sets of 8-10 reps. This variation targets the upper chest more than the flat bench press.

- Leg Press: 3 sets of 10 reps. Leg press machines are good for targeting the quads and glutes.

- Russian Twists: 3 sets of 15 reps per side. This exercise is great for oblique and core strength.

Intermediate routines can be done two to four times a week, depending on recovery and individual fitness goals.

Advanced Routine

Advanced routines are designed for those who have a solid fitness base and are looking to further challenge themselves. These routines often include higher intensity exercises, plyometrics, and supersets.

- Plyometric Box Jumps: 3 sets of 8-10 reps. Box jumps are excellent for developing explosive power in the legs.

- Superset: Barbell Squats and Deadlifts: 3 sets of 6-8 reps each. Performing these exercises back-to-back increases the intensity of the workout.

- Weighted Pull-Ups: 3 sets of 6-8 reps. Adding weight increases the difficulty of pull-ups.

- Dumbbell Snatch: 3 sets of 6-8 reps per arm. This is a full-body explosive movement that improves power and coordination.

- Superset: Dips and Push-Ups: 3 sets of 10-12 reps each. This combination works the chest and triceps intensely.

- Hanging Leg Raises: 3 sets of 10-15 reps. This exercise is challenging for the core, especially the lower abdominals.

Advanced routines can be performed three to five times a week, allowing for at least one day of rest between sessions for optimal muscle recovery and growth.

Each of these routines, from beginner to advanced, can be adjusted in terms of sets, reps, and weight to suit individual needs and progress. It's important to listen to the body and modify the workout as needed, ensuring consistent progression while avoiding injury.

The Upper/Lower Split

The upper/lower split is a dynamic and efficient approach to strength training and muscle building. This workout regimen involves dividing exercises into two primary categories: those that target the upper body and those that focus on the lower body. Typically, this split is structured over a four-day cycle, with two days dedicated to upper body workouts and two days for lower body workouts. The remaining days are reserved for rest or active recovery, making this split highly effective for both muscle development and recovery.

In an upper/lower split, the focus on upper body workouts involves exercises targeting the chest, back, shoulders, and arms. This concentrated effort on the upper half of the body during these sessions allows for intensive work on these muscle groups. The specific exercises might include bench presses, pull-ups, shoulder presses, and bicep curls, among others. Each of these exercises is designed to maximize muscle engagement in the upper body, contributing to improved strength and muscle definition.

The lower body days focus on the legs and glutes, involving exercises such as squats, deadlifts, lunges, and calf raises. These movements are crucial for building lower body strength and size. By dedicating entire sessions to the lower body, the split ensures that these major muscle groups receive the attention and workload necessary for growth and development.

One of the primary benefits of the upper/lower split is the focused training it offers. By concentrating on one half of the body at a time, it allows for a more intense workout session for each muscle group. This focused approach leads to better muscle fatigue and, consequently, more significant muscle growth and strength gains. It enables individuals to push their upper and lower body muscles to the limit, ensuring each workout's effectiveness.

Flexibility is another significant advantage of the upper/lower split. It can be tailored to fit various schedules and adjusted in frequency. For example, those with less time during the week can compress the split into a three-day cycle, focusing on full-body workouts. Alternatively, those who can dedicate more time can expand the split to a five or six-day cycle, allowing for more targeted exercises and increased volume.

The variety offered in the upper/lower split is crucial in preventing workout monotony. By alternating between upper and lower body workouts, individuals can incorporate a wide range of exercises, keeping the routine interesting and engaging. This variety not only maintains motivation but also ensures that all muscle groups are being worked effectively, reducing the risk of muscle imbalances.

Another critical aspect of the upper/lower split is recovery optimization. Each muscle group is given adequate time to rest and recover before being worked again. This recovery is essential for muscle repair and growth, as muscles grow during rest periods, not during the workouts themselves. By structuring the split to include rest or active recovery days, it promotes overall muscle recovery, reducing the risk of overtraining and injuries.

In conclusion, the upper/lower split is a versatile and effective approach to fitness training. Its structure allows for focused and intense workouts for both the upper and lower body, ensuring balanced muscle development and strength gains. The flexibility of the split makes it suitable for a wide range of individuals with different schedules and fitness goals. Its emphasis on recovery optimizes muscle growth and minimizes the risk of injury, making it a sustainable and effective workout regimen for anyone looking to improve their fitness.

Example Upper and Lower Body Workouts

The upper/lower split is a training method widely recognized for its efficiency in building strength and muscle mass. This approach divides workouts into two main categories: upper body and lower body routines. Each routine targets specific muscle groups, allowing for concentrated effort and optimal muscle development. Advanced techniques such as supersets, drop sets, and isolation exercises can further intensify these workouts, offering seasoned athletes a challenging and effective training regimen.

Upper Body Routine

The upper body routine primarily focuses on exercises that target the chest, back, shoulders, and arms. Key exercises in this routine include:

- Bench Presses: A fundamental exercise for developing chest strength and size. It also engages the triceps and shoulders. Performing 3-4 sets of 6-10 repetitions is ideal for muscle growth.

- Pull-Ups: Effective for working the upper back and biceps. Pull-ups also engage the core and improve overall upper body strength. Aim for 3 sets of as many reps as possible.

- Shoulder Presses: This exercise targets the deltoids and triceps. It's crucial for building shoulder strength and stability. 3 sets of 6-10 reps are recommended.

- Bicep Curls: Essential for building bicep strength and size. They also help in improving grip strength. Perform 3 sets of 8-12 reps.

These exercises should be performed with proper form and a weight that challenges the muscles while still allowing for the full range of motion. The upper body routine can be varied by including different variations of these exercises, such as incline bench presses or dumbbell curls, to target the muscles differently and avoid plateaus.

Lower Body Routine

The lower body routine focuses on exercises that target the quadriceps, hamstrings, glutes, and calves. Essential exercises for this routine include:

- Squats: A cornerstone exercise for lower body strength, targeting the quadriceps, hamstrings, and glutes. Aiming for 3-4 sets of 6-10 reps is effective for building strength and muscle.

- Deadlifts: Excellent for developing overall lower body strength, particularly in the hamstrings and glutes. Perform 3 sets of 6-8 reps.

- Lunges: Lunges are versatile and target the quadriceps, hamstrings, and glutes. They also help improve balance and stability. 3 sets of 10 reps per leg are recommended.

- Calf Raises: Specific for strengthening the calf muscles. Perform 3 sets of 12-15 reps.

These exercises should be executed with attention to form, ensuring that the movements are controlled and muscles are engaged correctly. Similar to the upper body routine, variations of these exercises can be incorporated to provide a comprehensive lower body workout.

Advanced Options

For those looking to further intensify their workouts, advanced techniques can be employed:

- Supersets: This involves performing two exercises back-to-back with no rest in between. For example, doing a set of bench presses immediately followed by a set of pull-ups.

- Drop Sets: Start with a heavier weight and perform reps until failure, then immediately drop to a lighter weight and continue to failure. This can be applied to exercises like bicep curls or squats.

- Isolation Exercises: These exercises target specific muscles or muscle groups. Examples include tricep pushdowns for the upper body and leg curls for the lower body.

These advanced techniques are beneficial for pushing muscles beyond their usual capacity, leading to increased strength and muscle gains. They should be incorporated judiciously to avoid overtraining and ensure proper recovery.

Incorporating these workouts into an upper/lower split allows for focused and effective training sessions, with each muscle group receiving adequate attention and recovery time. Whether following the basic routines or incorporating advanced techniques, the upper/lower split offers a structured path to achieving strength and muscle development goals.

Ideal Candidates for the Upper/Lower Split

The upper/lower split workout regimen is an excellent choice for a specific segment of the fitness population. This split, dividing workouts into upper and lower body sessions, is particularly well-suited for those who have moved beyond the beginner stage and are looking for more specialized training. It is also ideal for individuals with specific strength goals, athletes focused on symmetry, and those who have a moderate amount of time to dedicate to exercise.

Intermediate to advanced fitness enthusiasts find the upper/lower split particularly beneficial. Once the basic principles of strength training are mastered and the initial phase of muscle adaptation has occurred, these individuals often seek a more targeted approach to training. The upper/lower split allows them to concentrate more intensely on each muscle group, facilitating a deeper level of muscular development and strength gains. This split provides the opportunity to increase the volume and intensity of workouts for each specific muscle group, a key factor in advancing fitness levels.

Individuals with specific strength goals, such as increasing muscle mass or achieving certain strength benchmarks, will find the upper/lower split to be particularly conducive to their objectives. This split allows for a balanced approach to muscle development, ensuring that all major muscle groups are being worked evenly. By dividing the body into upper and lower segments, it ensures that both halves are receiving equal attention, avoiding the common pitfall of disproportionate development. This balance is crucial not only for aesthetic purposes but also for functional strength and injury prevention.

Athletes focused on symmetry also benefit greatly from the upper/lower split. Many sports require a balanced physique for optimal performance, and asymmetrical development can lead to imbalances and potential injuries. The upper/lower split ensures that athletes can target all muscle groups equally, promoting a symmetrical development that is often crucial in competitive sports. This focus on balanced development helps athletes improve their overall performance and reduce the risk of sport-specific injuries.

The upper/lower split is also suitable for those who have a moderate amount of time to dedicate to exercise. With four dedicated workout days - two upper body and two lower body - this split is efficient for those who can commit to a structured weekly routine but may not have the time for more frequent gym visits. This schedule allows for substantial workouts for each half of the body while providing enough rest and recovery time between sessions. It's an effective way to maximize workout time without requiring daily gym commitments, making it practical for those with busy lifestyles.

The upper/lower split is a versatile and effective training method that caters to a wide range of fitness enthusiasts. Its structured approach allows for focused and intense workouts, promoting significant strength gains and muscular development. Whether the goal is to build muscle, improve athletic performance, or simply achieve a balanced and symmetrical physique, the upper/lower split offers a practical and efficient pathway to these fitness objectives.

Example upper/lower split workouts

The upper/lower split workout regimen is a balanced and efficient approach to strength training, dividing workouts into upper and lower body sessions. This structure is particularly effective for those looking to enhance their muscle development, strength, and overall fitness. The split allows for focused training sessions, ensuring that each major muscle group receives the attention and intensity it needs for optimal growth and development.

For the upper body workout, the focus is on exercises that target the chest, shoulders, back, and arms. This could include a mix of compound movements that work multiple muscle groups simultaneously, providing a more efficient workout, and isolation exercises that focus on specific muscles. A typical upper body workout in the upper/lower split might look like this:

- Bench Press: A staple exercise for chest development. It also engages the triceps and shoulders. Start with 3 sets of 6-8 repetitions, focusing on lifting heavy while maintaining good form.

- Bent-Over Rows: Essential for building a strong back. Perform 3 sets of 6-8 reps, ensuring you pull with your back muscles rather than just your arms.

- Shoulder Press: Either with dumbbells or a barbell, this exercise targets the shoulders and triceps. Do 3 sets of 6-8 reps.

- Pull-Ups or Lat Pull-Downs: Great for the lats and overall upper body strength. Aim for 3 sets to failure if doing pull-ups or 3 sets of 8-10 reps for lat pull-downs.

- Bicep Curls: A focused movement for bicep development. Perform 3 sets of 8-12 reps.

- Tricep Dips or Tricep Pushdowns: Finish the workout with tricep-focused exercises, aiming for 3 sets of 8-12 reps.

For the lower body workout, the emphasis is on the quadriceps, hamstrings, glutes, and calves. These workouts typically involve heavy and intense leg exercises, capitalizing on the lower body's capacity for strength. An example of a lower body workout could include:

- Squats: The king of lower body exercises. Perform 3 sets of 6-8 reps, focusing on depth and form.

- Deadlifts: A full-body exercise that heavily involves the lower back, glutes, and hamstrings. Do 3 sets of 6-8 reps.

- Leg Press: Useful for targeting the quadriceps and glutes, especially when squats are too taxing. Aim for 3 sets of 10-12 reps.

- Lunges: Walking lunges or stationary lunges work the entire leg. Do 3 sets of 10 reps per leg.

- Leg Curls: Focus on the hamstrings with 3 sets of 10-12 reps.

- Calf Raises: Finish the session by targeting the calves with 3 sets of 15-20 reps.

These workouts in the upper/lower split allow for a balanced approach to strength training, ensuring that all major muscle groups are worked evenly and effectively. The split also provides enough flexibility for individuals to adjust exercises, sets, and reps according to their fitness levels and goals. For those looking to increase intensity, advanced techniques like supersets, drop sets, or increasing the weight can be incorporated.

Incorporating the upper/lower split into a weekly routine offers an effective way to build strength and muscle in a structured manner. By focusing on upper body exercises in one session and lower body exercises in another, it ensures comprehensive muscle development and adequate recovery time. This split is adaptable, allowing individuals to tailor their workouts to their specific needs, whether they're aiming to increase muscle mass, improve strength, or enhance overall fitness.

Push/Pull/Legs Split

The push/pull/legs split is a highly regarded and efficient workout structure that has gained substantial popularity in the fitness community. This method categorizes exercises based on primary movement patterns, creating a well-rounded and balanced training regimen. This split is particularly favored for its ability to optimize training while ensuring comprehensive muscle engagement.

The framework of the push/pull/legs split is straightforward yet effective. It divides workouts into three distinct categories: push workouts, pull workouts, and legs workouts. Push workouts focus on exercises that involve pushing movements, primarily targeting the chest, shoulders, and triceps. Typical exercises include bench presses, overhead presses, and push-ups. These workouts are designed to maximize the development of the anterior (front) upper body muscles.

Pull workouts, on the other hand, revolve around pulling movements. These sessions primarily engage the back, biceps, and forearms. Exercises commonly found in pull workouts include pull-ups, rows, and deadlifts. The emphasis is on the posterior (back) upper body muscles, ensuring a balanced development in conjunction with the push workouts.

Legs workouts are dedicated exclusively to the lower body. This category includes exercises that target the quadriceps, hamstrings, glutes, and calves. Key exercises in leg workouts include squats, lunges, and calf raises. These sessions are crucial for building lower body strength and symmetry with the upper body muscle groups.

Typically, the push/pull/legs split is executed over a three-day or six-day cycle. The three-day cycle is suitable for those with limited time or those who prefer longer recovery periods. It involves one day each for push, pull, and legs workouts, with rest or active recovery days in between. The six-day cycle doubles the frequency, allowing each muscle group to be worked twice a week. This higher frequency can lead to faster strength gains and muscle growth, but it requires a higher level of fitness and recovery capability.

One of the primary benefits of the push/pull/legs split is balanced muscle development. By categorizing workouts based on movement patterns, it ensures that all major muscle groups are worked evenly. This balanced approach prevents muscle imbalances and fosters a harmonious physique. It's particularly beneficial for those aiming for aesthetic improvements as well as functional strength.

Versatility is another significant advantage of this split. It can be adapted to various frequencies to accommodate different schedules and recovery needs. Whether an individual can commit to three days or six days of training per week, the push/pull/legs split can be modified accordingly. This flexibility makes it a viable option for a wide range of individuals, from busy professionals to dedicated athletes.

Focused intensity is a key characteristic of each workout day in the push/pull/legs split. By concentrating on specific muscle groups each session, it allows for a more intense and effective workout. This focus enhances muscle fatigue and growth within each group, leading to more efficient training sessions. It also allows for a higher volume of work for each muscle group, a critical factor for hypertrophy and strength gains.

Lastly, the split minimizes the chances of muscle overuse and fatigue. Since each muscle group is worked independently on different days, there's a reduced risk of overtraining. This separation allows for adequate recovery for each muscle group, which is crucial for muscle repair, growth, and overall workout effectiveness.

The push/pull/legs split is a structured approach to strength training, dividing workouts into three distinct categories – push, pull, and legs – each targeting specific muscle groups. This division allows for an intense focus on each muscle group, leading to more effective training sessions and balanced muscle development.

Push Workout

The push workout targets muscles involved in pushing movements, primarily the chest, shoulders, and triceps. This workout typically includes:

- Bench Press: A cornerstone exercise for chest development. It also engages the triceps and shoulders. Start with 3-4 sets of 6-10 repetitions, using a weight that challenges the muscles while maintaining proper form.

- Overhead Press: This exercise targets the shoulders (deltoids) and also works the triceps. Perform 3-4 sets of 6-10 reps, choosing a weight that allows for full range of motion.

- Tricep Dips: These focus on the triceps, and can be performed using parallel bars or a bench. Aim for 3 sets of 8-12 reps.

- Incline Bench Press: This variation targets the upper chest and shoulders more than the flat bench press. Perform 3 sets of 6-10 reps.

- Side Lateral Raises: Excellent for isolating the side deltoids. Do 3 sets of 10-15 reps using lighter weights for proper form.

The push workout effectively exhausts the upper body pushing muscles, leading to improved strength and size in these areas.

Pull Workout

The pull workout focuses on the upper body pulling muscles: the back, biceps, and forearms. Key exercises include:

- Deadlifts: A compound movement that targets the entire back, including the latissimus dorsi, rhomboids, and traps. Perform 3-4 sets of 6-8 reps with a challenging weight.

- Pull-Ups: Excellent for back and bicep development. Aim for 3 sets of as many reps as possible. If too difficult, assisted pull-ups or lat pull-downs can be substituted.

- Barbell Rows: Focus on the middle and lower back. Perform 3-4 sets of 6-10 reps, ensuring you're pulling with your back muscles.

- Bicep Curls: Can be done with dumbbells or a barbell. Aim for 3 sets of 8-12 reps.

- Face Pulls: Target the rear deltoids and upper back. Perform 3 sets of 12-15 reps.

The pull workout thoroughly works the back and bicep muscles, promoting balanced development with the pushing muscles.

Legs Workout

The legs workout is dedicated to the lower body, targeting the quadriceps, hamstrings, glutes, and calves. A typical legs workout includes:

- Squats: The most comprehensive lower body exercise. Perform 3-4 sets of 6-10 reps, focusing on depth and maintaining form.

- Lunges: Work the quads, hamstrings, and glutes. Do 3 sets of 10 reps per leg.

- Leg Press: An alternative or addition to squats, targeting the quads and glutes. Aim for 3 sets of 10-12 reps.

- Romanian Deadlifts: Focus on the hamstrings and glutes. Perform 3 sets of 8-10 reps.

- Calf Raises: Essential for developing the calf muscles. Do 3 sets of 12-15 reps.

The legs workout ensures that the lower body is not neglected, providing a balanced approach to full-body development.

Each of these workouts in the push/pull/legs split allows for targeted muscle development and strength gains. By focusing on specific muscle groups in each session, the split ensures comprehensive development across all major muscle groups. The routine can be adapted in terms of the number of sets, repetitions, and weights used to suit individual fitness levels and goals.

Ideal Candidates for the Push/Pull/Legs Split

The push/pull/legs split is a highly versatile workout regimen well-suited for certain types of trainees due to its specific structure and intense focus on different muscle groups. This split is ideal for intermediate and advanced trainees, individuals with flexible schedules, and those with goal-specific training targets such as building strength, hypertrophy, or muscle definition.

Intermediate and Advanced Trainees

Intermediate and advanced trainees often reach a point in their fitness journey where generalized workouts no longer yield the same level of results as before. These individuals require a more specific and intense focus on each muscle group to continue progressing. The push/pull/legs split meets this need perfectly, as it allows for an intense workout of each muscle group before moving on to the next. This split provides the opportunity to focus on heavier lifts and more complex movements that are crucial for continued muscle development and strength gains. Since each workout day is dedicated to a specific set of muscles, it's easier to target weaknesses and work on specific areas for balanced, overall development.

Individuals with a Flexible Schedule

The push/pull/legs split is highly adaptable, making it suitable for individuals with varying schedules. For those who can commit to a six-day workout cycle, this split allows each muscle group to be worked twice a week, accelerating progress in strength and hypertrophy. Alternatively, for those with tighter schedules or who require more recovery time, the split can be adjusted to a three-day cycle. This flexibility is a significant advantage, as it allows individuals to tailor their workout routine to their lifestyle without compromising the effectiveness of their training program. The ability to adjust the frequency also means that the split can accommodate changes in an individual's life, be it due to work, family commitments, or other responsibilities.

Goal-Specific Trainees

Individuals with specific fitness goals such as building strength, increasing muscle size (hypertrophy), or enhancing overall muscle definition find the push/pull/legs split particularly beneficial. This workout structure allows for focused and intense training sessions that are key to these goals. For strength and hypertrophy, the split supports high-volume and high-intensity workouts, crucial for stimulating muscle growth and strength improvement. The separation of muscle groups ensures that each group is thoroughly exhausted in its workout, an essential factor in muscle hypertrophy.

Furthermore, for those focusing on muscle definition, this split allows for targeted exercises that can sculpt and define various muscle groups. The ability to concentrate on specific areas in each workout ensures that all muscles are developed evenly, contributing to a more defined and aesthetic physique.

The Bro Split

The "bro split" stands as a classic, time-tested approach to strength training and bodybuilding. Its roots run deep in the fitness community, where it has been embraced for its intense focus on individual muscle groups. The bro split dedicates each day of the week to training a specific muscle group, typically spread over five to six days. This structure allows for highly focused and intense workouts for each muscle group, providing ample time for recovery before the same group is worked again.

The bro split's primary appeal lies in its intense muscle focus. This split allows for a high volume and intensity of training for each muscle group. For example, a typical bro split routine might dedicate one day entirely to chest exercises, another to back, and so on. This approach ensures that each muscle group is thoroughly worked during its dedicated session, leading to significant muscle fatigue and subsequent growth. This focus is particularly beneficial for those looking to increase muscle size and definition, as it allows for targeted development of each muscle group.

Simplicity is another key advantage of the bro split. Its straightforward structure is easy to understand and follow, making it an attractive option for both beginners and experienced gym-goers. This simplicity also aids in maintaining a routine, as there's no confusion about what muscle group to work on any given day. For beginners, it provides a clear roadmap for navigating the gym, and for the experienced, it allows for a well-structured approach to their training.

Customization is a significant aspect of the bro split. It allows for a high degree of personalization in choosing exercises for each muscle group. Depending on individual preferences, goals, and needs, exercises can be selected to target different aspects of each muscle group. For instance, on chest day, one could focus on flat bench presses, incline presses, and flyes, tailoring the workout to specific chest areas.

One of the most critical aspects of the bro split is the recovery time it affords each muscle group. By working each muscle group intensely once a week, the split provides a full week of recovery before that group is worked again. This extended recovery period is beneficial for muscle growth and repair, as muscles need time to recover and grow after being subjected to intense training. It's during this recovery period that the actual process of muscle building occurs.

The bro split's focus on one muscle group per day also allows for a more extended workout for each group. This can lead to increased muscle exhaustion and, consequently, growth. For example, dedicating an entire session to the back allows for a variety of exercises targeting different back parts, such as the latissimus dorsi, rhomboids, and trapezius muscles. This variety ensures comprehensive development of the muscle group and can lead to more pronounced muscle gains.

Additionally, the bro split's structure aids in preventing burnout and overtraining. By concentrating on one muscle group per session, the risk of overworking a muscle group is significantly reduced. This approach allows for more focused energy and effort during each workout, as only one major muscle group is being taxed per session.

However, the bro split requires a significant time commitment, as it typically involves training five to six days a week. This commitment can be challenging for those with busy schedules or limited time for gym sessions. Despite this, for those who can dedicate the necessary time, the bro split offers a highly effective way to build muscle and strength.

Example Workout Routine

The bro split routine is a classic approach in bodybuilding and strength training circles, targeting one major muscle group each day of the week. This approach allows for an intense focus on each muscle group, providing ample time for recovery before the same group is worked again. A sample weekly bro split routine can be structured as follows:

Monday: Chest Day

- Bench Press: Begin with 3-4 sets of 6-8 reps. The bench press is a staple in chest development, targeting the pectorals, triceps, and front deltoids.

- Incline Dumbbell Press: Perform 3 sets of 8-10 reps. This exercise focuses on the upper chest, promoting a balanced chest development.

- Chest Flyes: Do 3 sets of 10-12 reps. Flyes help to stretch and isolate the chest muscles, enhancing muscle definition.

Tuesday: Back Day

- Pull-Ups: Aim for 3-4 sets to failure. Pull-ups are excellent for overall back development, particularly targeting the latissimus dorsi.

- Bent-Over Rows: Complete 3 sets of 6-8 reps. This exercise strengthens the middle back muscles and contributes to overall back thickness.

- Lat Pulldowns: Do 3 sets of 8-10 reps. Lat pulldowns focus on the width of the back, particularly the lats.

Wednesday: Shoulders Day

- Overhead Press: Start with 3-4 sets of 6-8 reps. The overhead press is crucial for building overall shoulder strength and size.

- Lateral Raises: Perform 3 sets of 10-12 reps. Lateral raises target the side deltoids, essential for shoulder width and definition.

- Front Raises: Do 3 sets of 10-12 reps. This exercise targets the front deltoids, rounding out shoulder development.

Thursday: Arms Day

- Bicep Curls: Perform 3 sets of 8-10 reps. Bicep curls are fundamental for building arm size and strength.

- Tricep Extensions: Complete 3 sets of 8-10 reps. Tricep extensions target the triceps muscles, crucial for overall arm development.

- Hammer Curls: Do 3 sets of 10-12 reps. Hammer curls focus on the brachialis and brachioradialis, enhancing arm thickness and strength.

Friday: Legs Day

- Squats: Begin with 3-4 sets of 6-8 reps. Squats are essential for overall leg development, particularly the quadriceps and glutes.

- Deadlifts: Perform 3 sets of 6-8 reps. Deadlifts target the entire posterior chain, including the hamstrings, glutes, and lower back.

- Leg Presses: Complete 3 sets of 10-12 reps. The leg press is a great complement to squats, targeting the quads and glutes with less strain on the lower back.

Saturday: Rest or Optional Focus on a Weak Muscle Group

This day can be used for rest or to focus on a weaker muscle group that needs additional attention. If choosing to train, select 2-3 exercises for the targeted muscle group and perform a moderate workout, being mindful not to overtrain.

Sunday: Rest

Dedicate this day to complete rest, allowing your body to recover, repair, and grow stronger. Rest is a critical component of any training routine, particularly one as intense as the bro split.

This sample weekly bro split routine offers a comprehensive approach to muscle building, with each day dedicated to enhancing a specific muscle group. It's crucial to ensure proper form and adequate recovery between sets and exercises. Additionally, listen to your body and make adjustments as needed based on your recovery and overall fitness progress.

Ideal Candidates for the Bro Split

The bro split, known for its intense focus on individual muscle groups, is a workout regimen that resonates with specific segments of the fitness community. Its structure, which dedicates each day to a different muscle group, makes it particularly suitable for certain types of individuals, such as bodybuilders, experienced lifters, those with flexible schedules, and recovery-oriented trainees.

Bodybuilders and Muscle Builders

The bro split is ideal for bodybuilders and those focusing on muscle hypertrophy and definition. This split's structure allows for an intensive workout on each muscle group, leading to significant muscle fatigue and growth. By dedicating an entire day to one muscle group, individuals can perform a high volume of exercises targeting various aspects of that muscle, which is crucial for hypertrophy. The bro split also allows for a focus on muscle definition. The ability to concentrate on one muscle group at a time enables lifters to perform isolation exercises that enhance muscle shape and definition, a key goal in bodybuilding.

Experienced Lifters

Experienced lifters, who already have a solid foundation in strength training, find the bro split particularly effective. These individuals are typically capable of handling high-volume and high-intensity workouts that the bro split demands. Having developed a base level of strength and muscle endurance, they can benefit from the intensive nature of the bro split, which can lead to further strength gains and muscle development. Experienced lifters often have the technique and stamina necessary to withstand the rigors of this type of training, making the bro split a suitable choice for their advanced training needs.

Those with Flexible Schedules

The bro split is best suited for individuals who can dedicate five to six days a week to their workout routine. Due to its structure, the bro split requires a significant time commitment, with each workout day focusing on a different muscle group. This frequency is essential for the split's effectiveness, as it ensures that each muscle group is thoroughly worked each week. Individuals with the flexibility to commit to this type of schedule will find the bro split to be a practical and efficient way to structure their workouts.

Recovery-Oriented Trainees

Trainees who require or prefer longer recovery periods for each muscle group will find the bro split beneficial. Since each muscle group is worked intensely only once a week, there is ample time for recovery before that group is targeted again. This extended recovery time can be advantageous for muscle repair and growth. For individuals who need more time to recover due to their physiological makeup, age, or other factors, the bro split provides the necessary rest period for each muscle

The 5x5 Split

The 5x5 training program is a paradigm of strength training, valued for its straightforward yet highly effective approach. Centering on five sets of five repetitions of key compound lifts, this program is not just about building muscle; it's a comprehensive method to enhance overall strength and athletic performance. The 5x5 program is a testament to the principle that in simplicity lies power. This regimen revolves around a select few compound exercises, each performed with heavy weights. The core idea is to engage multiple muscle groups simultaneously, making every session both time-efficient and potent.

Compound exercises are the linchpin of the 5x5 program. These movements, such as squats, deadlifts, bench presses, and overhead presses, work several muscle groups at once. Unlike isolation exercises that target individual muscles, compound movements recruit large muscle areas, offering a more holistic approach to strength building. This method not only accelerates muscle growth but also enhances functional strength – the kind of strength that is useful in everyday life.

Squats, for instance, engage the quadriceps, hamstrings, glutes, lower back, and core, making them an incredibly effective lower body exercise.

The deadlift, another staple of the 5x5 program, works almost every major muscle group, including the back, glutes, legs, and core. The bench press and overhead press are critical for developing the upper body, targeting the chest, shoulders, and triceps. These exercises combined provide a balanced workout that strengthens the entire body.

A key feature of the 5x5 program is its emphasis on progressive overload, a crucial principle in strength training. Progressive overload involves gradually increasing the weight lifted to challenge the muscles continuously. This approach is critical for muscle growth and strength improvement. In the context of the 5x5 program, once an individual can complete five sets of five reps with a certain weight, they increase the weight slightly in the next workout. This gradual increase ensures steady progress and minimizes the risk of injury.

The 5x5 program is also marked by its simplicity, both in terms of the exercises involved and its implementation. With only a handful of exercises to focus on, it's easier for individuals to track their progress and maintain consistency. This simplicity is especially beneficial for beginners who can often be overwhelmed by more complex routines. For the experienced lifter, the straightforward nature of the program provides a clear structure for continued development.

However, the simplicity of the 5x5 program doesn't imply that it's easy. The workouts can be quite challenging, particularly as the weights increase. The five sets of five reps scheme requires a significant amount of physical and mental endurance. This aspect of the program builds not just muscle, but also grit and determination, qualities that are invaluable in any fitness journey.

The 5x5 program is also adaptable. While the traditional 5x5 split focuses on three workouts per week, it can be adjusted according to individual needs and schedules. For example, someone with more time and recovery capability might add a fourth day focusing on accessory exercises or additional cardiovascular work. Conversely, for someone pressed for time, the program can be condensed into two longer workouts per week.

This training regimen is particularly well-suited for those looking to gain strength in a structured and measurable way. It is ideal for beginners to intermediate lifters, though advanced lifters can also benefit significantly by returning to this fundamental strength-building approach. The 5x5 program is not just about lifting weights; it's about building a solid foundation upon which other fitness goals can be achieved.

In essence, the 5x5 program is a powerful tool in the arsenal of strength training. Its focus on compound movements, progressive overload, and simplicity makes it an effective and efficient method for building strength and muscle. This program proves that sometimes, the most straightforward approaches can be the most impactful, providing a clear path to greater strength and overall fitness.

Example 5x5 Workouts

The 5x5 workout program, renowned for its simplicity and effectiveness, revolves around two primary workout routines – Workout A and Workout B. These routines are alternated three times a week, focusing on major compound movements that engage multiple muscle groups. The essence of the 5x5 program lies in its structured approach, performing five sets of five reps for each exercise, except for deadlifts, which due to their intensity, are typically performed for one set of five reps.

Workout A

- Squat: The squat is a fundamental exercise in the 5x5 program. It targets the quadriceps, hamstrings, glutes, lower back, and core. For the 5x5 routine, you perform five sets of five reps. The focus should be on maintaining proper form, keeping the back straight, and driving through the heels. As a full-body compound movement, it not only builds lower body strength but also contributes to overall muscle growth and development.

- Bench Press: Next in Workout A is the bench press, which primarily works the chest muscles (pectorals), as well as the triceps and shoulders (deltoids). Again, five sets of five reps are performed. Proper form includes lying flat on the bench, feet firmly on the ground, and controlling the barbell as it's lowered to the chest and pushed back up. The bench press is key for upper body strength and is a staple in strength training.

- Barbell Row: The barbell row focuses on the upper back, including the latissimus dorsi, rhomboids, and trapezius muscles, as well as the biceps. It's crucial for maintaining balance in the body's musculature, countering the pushing movements of the bench press. Perform five sets of five reps, maintaining a bent-over position with a straight back, pulling the barbell towards the lower ribs, and then lowering it under control.

Workout B

- Squat: As in Workout A, the squat is also the first exercise in Workout B, highlighting its importance in the program. The same approach is followed – five sets of five reps, focusing on depth, form, and control. Consistent performance of squats is crucial for lower body strength and overall athletic ability.

- Overhead Press: The overhead press, or military press, targets the shoulders, triceps, and upper back. This exercise is performed standing, pressing the barbell from shoulder height above the head. Five sets of five reps are done, ensuring that each rep involves a full range of motion from shoulders to lockout above the head. The overhead press is essential for building strong, functional shoulders and arms.

- Deadlift: The deadlift is a powerful compound exercise that targets the entire posterior chain, including the hamstrings, glutes, lower and upper back. Due to its intensity, only one set of five reps is performed in the 5x5 program. Proper form is crucial to avoid injury – keeping the back straight, lifting with the legs and hips, and keeping the barbell close to the body throughout the lift.

In both Workout A and Workout B, the weights used should be challenging yet manageable to complete all sets and reps with proper form. The 5x5 program is designed for progressive overload, meaning that as you grow stronger, you should gradually increase the weight used in each exercise. This progression is key to the effectiveness of the 5x5 program, driving consistent strength and muscle gains.

These workouts encapsulate the essence of strength training – focusing on major compound movements, challenging the body, and promoting growth. The simplicity of the 5x5 program makes it highly effective, ensuring a balanced approach to building foundational strength.

Benefits of Strength-Focused Splits

Strength-focused workout splits, particularly the renowned 5x5 program, offer a plethora of benefits for a wide demographic, ranging from beginners to seasoned athletes. These splits, known for their simplicity and effectiveness, are designed to build foundational strength that is applicable to both sports and daily activities. They provide a structured pathway for increasing muscle strength, enhancing bone and joint health, boosting metabolism, and improving athletic performance.

One of the most significant benefits of strength-focused splits like the 5x5 program is the increased muscle strength. This type of training regimen emphasizes heavy lifting with compound movements, which are key to developing overall muscular strength. Compound exercises such as squats, deadlifts, and bench presses target multiple muscle groups simultaneously, allowing for a more efficient strength-building workout. Increased muscle strength is not only beneficial for enhancing physical appearance but is also crucial in improving daily functional abilities, such as lifting heavy objects, pushing or pulling items, and maintaining overall body stability.

Another crucial benefit of these workout splits is their positive impact on bone and joint health. Strength training is known to enhance bone density, which is especially important as one ages. Regularly performing weight-bearing exercises helps in combating age-related bone loss, reducing the risk of osteoporosis, and other bone-related conditions. Furthermore, by strengthening the muscles around the joints, these workouts contribute to joint stability, which can help prevent injuries and improve overall joint health.

Metabolic boost is another key advantage of engaging in strength-focused workout splits. Strength training has been shown to elevate metabolism, aiding in fat loss and muscle maintenance. This metabolic increase occurs because muscle tissue burns more calories at rest compared to fat tissue. Therefore, by increasing muscle mass through strength training, one can elevate their resting metabolic rate, making it easier to maintain a healthy body weight or lose fat if that's a personal goal.

Improved athletic performance is a direct outcome of engaging in a strength-focused training regimen. Strength gains achieved through these workouts translate to better performance in almost every athletic endeavor, be it running, swimming, cycling, or team sports. Enhanced muscle strength and endurance allow athletes to perform at a higher level, improve their technique, and reduce the risk of sport-related injuries.

The 5x5 workout split, in particular, is excellent for strength training beginners due to its straightforward approach. This program simplifies strength training into a manageable format, focusing on a few key exercises and requiring only three workouts per week. For someone new to strength training, this simplicity eliminates the often overwhelming complexity of more intricate workout routines, providing a clear and concise pathway to gaining strength and confidence in the gym.

Athletes, regardless of their sport, can benefit immensely from the 5x5 split. For competitive sports, a strong foundation of muscular strength is often a prerequisite for peak performance. The 5x5 program offers a focused approach to building this foundation, ensuring athletes develop the strength needed to excel in their respective sports.

Individuals with limited time find the 5x5 split ideal. Since the program is designed for efficiency, requiring only three days a week, it's suitable for those with busy schedules. Each workout in the 5x5 program is concise yet effective, focusing on a few compound exercises that provide a full-body workout in a relatively short period.

Lastly, the 5x5 split is suitable for anyone seeking to improve their overall functional fitness and core strength. This program not only builds muscle in the traditional sense but also enhances the body's ability to perform everyday activities more efficiently and with less risk of injury. The focus on compound movements ensures that the core and stabilizing muscles are engaged, which is crucial for overall functional strength.

In summary, strength-focused splits, and particularly the 5x5 program, are beneficial for a wide range of individuals. They offer a structured approach to increasing muscle strength, enhancing bone and joint health, boosting metabolism, and improving athletic performance. These splits are ideal for beginners, athletes, individuals with limited time, and those seeking functional strength, making them a versatile tool in achieving various fitness goals.

Hybrid and Custom Splits

Hybrid and custom workout splits represent an innovative approach to fitness training, offering unparalleled flexibility and personalization. These types of splits are tailored to individual needs, blending elements from traditional workout splits to create a unique fitness regimen. This approach is particularly beneficial for individuals with specific goals, varied interests, or unique scheduling needs.

The concept of hybrid and custom splits is rooted in the idea that no one-size-fits-all solution exists for fitness training. Every individual has unique goals, preferences, body types, and lifestyles, all of which should be considered when designing a workout plan. Hybrid splits allow for the combination of different training styles and methodologies. For example, someone might combine elements of a body part split (like the bro split) with full-body workout days. This could mean dedicating specific days to focus intensely on one muscle group while incorporating full-body workouts on other days for balanced development.

Designing a custom split requires a thoughtful assessment of personal goals. For instance, someone aiming to build strength might focus more on heavy compound exercises, whereas someone interested in muscle toning might incorporate a mix of weightlifting and high-repetition training. Endurance enhancement might call for integrating cardiovascular exercises, while weight loss could involve a combination of strength training and high-intensity interval training (HIIT). Understanding these goals is crucial in shaping the structure of the workout split.

An individual's lifestyle and time availability play a significant role in designing a custom split. For those with demanding jobs or family commitments, a workout split needs to be efficient and flexible. For example, a busy professional might opt for shorter, more intense workout sessions or fewer training days with longer workouts. Similarly, someone with a more flexible schedule might choose a split that allows for more frequent but shorter sessions.

Recovery capability is another critical factor. The workout split should provide enough time for rest and muscle recovery, which is essential for growth and preventing overtraining. This consideration might lead to alternating between intense workout days and lighter or active recovery days.

The incorporation of varied training styles is a hallmark of hybrid and custom splits. This variety not only keeps the workouts interesting and challenging but also ensures that all major muscle groups are worked. For instance, someone might combine powerlifting exercises for strength with bodybuilding techniques for hypertrophy and some elements of functional training for overall fitness.

Ensuring comprehensive development of all muscle groups is essential in a hybrid or custom split. This means that while the split might focus on certain areas or goals, it should still provide a balanced workout regimen. For example, if someone's primary focus is on upper body strength, they should still incorporate lower body and core exercises to prevent imbalances and maintain overall fitness.

Hybrid and custom splits also allow for specific tailoring to address individual weaknesses or preferences. For example, if someone has a weaker lower back, they can incorporate specific exercises to strengthen that area. Similarly, if someone prefers certain types of exercises or equipment, those can be integrated into their custom plan.

Flexibility in adjusting the split over time is another advantage. As individuals progress in their fitness journey, their goals and needs might change. A custom or hybrid split can be easily modified to accommodate these changes, whether it's increasing the intensity, changing the focus, or incorporating new exercises.

In summary, hybrid and custom workout splits offer a personalized approach to fitness training. By blending elements from different splits and tailoring them to individual needs and goals, these splits provide a flexible and effective way to achieve fitness objectives. Whether it's building strength, enhancing muscle tone, improving endurance, or losing weight, hybrid and custom splits offer a tailored pathway to reach these goals while ensuring a balanced and comprehensive approach to physical development.

Examples of Hybrid Splits

Hybrid workout splits represent a modern and adaptable approach to fitness, combining elements from various established training methods to suit individual needs and goals. These hybrid splits provide the flexibility to focus on specific areas while maintaining a holistic approach to fitness. Let's delve into some examples of hybrid splits and how they can be structured.

Upper/Lower + Full Body Split

This hybrid split merges the focus of an upper/lower split with the comprehensive approach of full-body workouts. In a typical week, a trainee might alternate between upper/lower body days and full-body workout days. This structure allows for concentrated effort on specific muscle groups during the upper/lower days, while full-body days ensure all muscle groups are engaged within the same session.

For example, the week might begin with an upper body workout on Monday, focusing on exercises like bench presses and pull-ups. Tuesday could then shift to a lower body workout with squats and deadlifts. Wednesday might be a rest or active recovery day, followed by a full-body workout on Thursday, incorporating a mix of upper and lower body exercises. The cycle could then repeat or mix in additional rest days, depending on the individual's recovery needs and schedule.

Push/Pull/Legs + Bro Split Hybrid

This hybrid split combines the push/pull/legs framework with elements of the bro split, dedicating specific days to individual muscle groups. This structure allows for a balance between focused muscle group training and comprehensive workouts. For example, a week might start with a push workout (chest, shoulders, triceps) on Monday, followed by a pull workout (back, biceps) on Tuesday, and a legs workout (quadriceps, hamstrings, calves) on Wednesday.

The latter part of the week could then shift to a bro split approach, with Thursday dedicated to chest, Friday to back, and Saturday to arms. This hybrid split allows for intense focus on each muscle group while still maintaining the balanced approach of the push/pull/legs split.

5x5 + Functional Training Split

This hybrid combines the strength-focused 5x5 program, known for its simplicity and effectiveness in building strength, with functional training exercises to enhance athletic performance. The 5x5 portion of the workout, which includes exercises like squats, deadlifts, and bench presses, could be performed three days a week – for example, Monday, Wednesday, and Friday.

On alternate days, functional training exercises could be incorporated. These exercises focus on movements that mimic daily activities or sports-specific movements, improving overall athletic ability and functional strength. Such workouts might include kettlebell swings, medicine ball throws, or plyometric exercises. This combination ensures the development of raw strength while also enhancing agility, balance, and coordination.

Endurance and Strength Split

This hybrid split is ideal for those looking to balance endurance training with strength training. It's particularly suitable for athletes in sports that require both strength and endurance, such as obstacle course racing or triathlon. In this split, endurance training sessions (such as running, cycling, or swimming) could be alternated with strength training workouts.

A typical week might include endurance training on Monday, Wednesday, and Friday, focusing on different aspects such as speed, distance, and recovery pace. Strength training sessions on Tuesday, Thursday, and Saturday would then focus on full-body strength workouts, ensuring that all major muscle groups are targeted. This split allows for the development of both cardiovascular endurance and muscular strength, contributing to overall athletic performance and fitness.

In summary, hybrid workout splits offer a versatile approach to fitness training, allowing individuals to tailor their workouts to their specific goals and preferences. Whether the goal is to build muscle, enhance athletic performance, or achieve a balance of strength and endurance, hybrid splits provide a structured yet flexible framework to achieve these objectives. These examples demonstrate the adaptability of hybrid splits, accommodating a wide range of fitness levels and goals.

The Benefits of Personalized Splits

Personalized workout splits, encompassing both hybrid and custom splits, represent a cutting-edge approach in the fitness realm. These splits are designed to cater directly to individual needs, preferences, and goals, offering a multitude of benefits that standard, one-size-fits-all routines fail to provide. The primary advantages of these personalized splits include targeted results, adaptability, enhanced motivation, and the potential for holistic development.

Targeted Results

One of the most compelling reasons for adopting a personalized workout split is the ability to achieve targeted results. Each individual has unique fitness goals, whether it's building muscle, increasing endurance, losing weight, or improving athletic performance. A personalized split allows for the creation of a workout routine that directly aligns with these specific objectives. For instance, someone aiming for muscle hypertrophy might focus more on weightlifting and high-volume workouts, while an endurance athlete would integrate more cardiovascular exercises into their split. This tailored approach ensures that every minute spent in the gym is optimized towards achieving the desired outcome.

Adaptability

Personalized workout splits offer unparalleled adaptability. Life is dynamic, and circumstances can change rapidly, impacting one's ability to stick to a rigid workout schedule. Custom splits can be easily modified to accommodate changes in lifestyle, time availability, or fitness level. For example, if an individual's work schedule becomes more demanding, the split can be adjusted to shorter, more intense workouts, or if an injury occurs, the routine can be altered to focus on recovery and exercises that do not strain the affected area. This flexibility is not just a matter of convenience; it's crucial for maintaining consistent progress in the face of life's unpredictable nature.

Enhanced Motivation

Customization in workout routines keeps the training process engaging and relevant, which is vital for sustained motivation. Doing the same exercises week after week can lead to boredom and a plateau in progress. Personalized splits allow for variety and creativity in workouts, keeping the individual engaged and challenged. This might involve mixing different types of training, such as incorporating elements of powerlifting into a bodybuilding routine or blending yoga and mobility work into a strength training program. This variety not only makes workouts more enjoyable but also ensures that different aspects of fitness are being developed.

Holistic Development

Personalized splits offer the potential for a well-rounded approach to fitness. Standard workout routines often focus on specific goals, like muscle building or cardiovascular endurance, which can lead to imbalances in development. Custom splits, on the other hand, can be designed to address all aspects of fitness – strength, endurance, flexibility, and balance – leading to a more holistic development. This approach is crucial for overall health and wellness and can significantly reduce the risk of injuries that often result from imbalances or overemphasis on certain types of training.

Ideal Candidates for Hybrid and Custom Splits

- Experienced Gym-Goers: Individuals who have spent considerable time in the gym and understand their bodies and fitness needs are ideal candidates for hybrid and custom splits. These individuals have the knowledge to mix different training styles effectively, tailoring their routines to their evolving goals and preferences.

- Goal-Specific Athletes: Athletes training for specific sports or events require workout routines that address the particular demands of their sport. Personalized splits allow these athletes to focus on the aspects of fitness that will most enhance their performance in their chosen sport, be it strength, speed, agility, or endurance.

- People with Unique Schedules: Those whose lifestyles demand flexibility in their workout routines can greatly benefit from custom splits. Be it working parents, traveling professionals, or students balancing studies and fitness, personalized splits offer the adaptability needed to fit workouts into diverse and often changing schedules.

- Fitness Enthusiasts Seeking Variety: For those who enjoy exploring different aspects of fitness and dislike the monotony of standard routines, personalized splits offer an opportunity to diversify their training. This might involve experimenting with new exercises, incorporating different training methodologies, or adjusting the routine to align with changing fitness interests.

Personalized workout splits offer a range of benefits that standard workout programs often fail to provide. Their ability to deliver targeted results, adaptability to changing circumstances, enhancement of motivation through customization, and the potential for holistic development make them an excellent choice for a wide array of individuals. From experienced gym-goers and specific-goal athletes to people with unique schedules and fitness enthusiasts seeking variety, personalized workout splits present a flexible and effective solution for achieving diverse fitness goals.

Navigating the Complexities of Workout Splits

In the realm of fitness and bodybuilding, workout splits are a fundamental concept, often surrounded by questions and misconceptions. This chapter aims to provide clarity and guidance on navigating the complexities of workout splits, offering answers to frequently asked questions, debunking common misconceptions, and providing tips to avoid typical mistakes.

Frequently Asked Questions

- Changing Workout Splits: How often one should change their workout split depends on several factors, including progress, boredom, and adaptation. Generally, it's advisable to change your split every 8-12 weeks to prevent plateaus and keep the training stimulus fresh. However, if a split is still yielding results and remains enjoyable, it's perfectly fine to stick with it longer.

- Cardio on Rest Days: Incorporating light to moderate cardio on rest days can be beneficial. It keeps the body active and can aid in recovery by increasing blood flow to the muscles. However, it's important to ensure that this doesn't compromise recovery by being too intense or lengthy.

- Necessity of Specific Splits for Results: While workout splits can be highly effective, they are not the only way to achieve fitness results. The key to success in any training program is consistency, proper nutrition, and a workout plan that aligns with one's goals, whether it's a split routine or a full-body approach.

- Determining the Right Split: Choosing the right workout split involves considering factors such as fitness goals, experience level, schedule, and personal preferences. It's essential to select a split that not only aligns with your goals but is also realistic in terms of your time commitment and enjoyment.

- Combining Different Workout Splits: Yes, it's possible to combine different types of workout splits. This approach, often seen in hybrid splits, allows for more customization and can address specific training goals or preferences. For example, one could combine elements of a push/pull/legs split with full-body workouts.

Debunking Common Misconceptions

- More Gym Time Equals Better Results: Quality over quantity is crucial in fitness. Longer or more frequent gym sessions don't necessarily lead to better results and can sometimes lead to overtraining or burnout.

- Sticking to One Workout Split: While consistency is important, it's not mandatory to stick to one workout split indefinitely. Changing your split can provide new challenges and stimuli to the muscles, aiding in continued progress.

- Heavier Weights Are Always Better: While lifting heavy is important for strength and muscle building, it's not the only way to achieve results. Different rep ranges and intensities have their place in a well-rounded fitness program.

- Rest Days for Complete Inactivity: Rest days are essential for recovery, but they don't necessarily mean complete inactivity. Active recovery, such as light cardio, stretching, or yoga, can be beneficial.

Tips to Avoid Common Mistakes in Workout Splits

- Not Allowing Adequate Recovery: Underestimating the importance of rest can lead to overtraining and hinder progress. It's essential to include rest days in your split and listen to your body for signs of fatigue.

- Ignoring Nutrition and Hydration: Both play a crucial role in supporting your workout split. Proper nutrition fuels your workouts and aids in recovery, while staying hydrated is key for overall health and exercise performance.

- Lack of Consistency: Sticking to a workout routine is fundamental for seeing results. Consistency trumps perfection, and being regular with your workouts is more important than waiting for the 'perfect' time or conditions.

- Imbalanced Training: Focusing too much on certain muscle groups and neglecting others can lead to imbalances and injuries. Ensure your split addresses all major muscle groups evenly.

- Ignoring Form and Technique: Proper form and technique are essential for preventing injuries and getting the most out of your exercises. Always prioritize form over the amount of weight lifted.

Fine-Tuning Your Workout Split

- Listening to Your Body: Be attentive to what your body tells you. If you feel overly fatigued or experience pain (beyond normal muscle soreness), it may be time to adjust your split or intensity.

- Seeking Professional Guidance: Especially when starting a new split or if you hit a plateau, consulting with a fitness professional can provide valuable insights and guidance.

Incorporating Feedback into Your Routine

- Adapting to Changes: Be prepared to modify your workout split in response to changes in your fitness levels, goals, or life circumstances. Flexibility in your approach will help maintain progress.

- Learning from Experience: Both your own experiences and those of others can be insightful. Continually refine your approach based on what you learn about your body and its response to different training stimuli.

In navigating the world of workout splits, understanding these facets is crucial. By gaining clarity on these aspects, individuals can tailor their fitness routines to be more effective, enjoyable, and aligned with

Part 3: Mental Aspects

Mental Health and Achieving Physical Goals

The significance of mental health in achieving physical goals, especially in high-discipline fields like bodybuilding, is well-documented. Sports psychologists have long recognized the interplay between mental well-being and physical performance. Dr. Jim Taylor, in his work on sports psychology, asserts, "Physical training is what builds the body, but mental training is what directs it to perform effectively" (Taylor, 2009). This perspective is particularly relevant in bodybuilding, where the mental discipline required can be as intense as the physical training.

Achieving peak physical condition in bodybuilding demands not just rigorous training and strict dieting but also a high level of mental stamina. Mental health issues, such as stress, anxiety, or lack of motivation, can significantly hinder an athlete's training progress and performance. A study published in the Journal of Applied Sport Psychology found a direct correlation between athletes' mental health and their performance, indicating that better mental health leads to improved physical performance (Gould & Dieffenbach, 2002).

In bodybuilding, where the focus is often on physical appearance and strength, the importance of mental health can sometimes be overlooked. However, maintaining mental well-being is crucial for sustaining the motivation, focus, and discipline necessary to achieve challenging physical goals. This includes managing the psychological stress of competition, coping with the pressures of strict training regimens, and maintaining a positive self-image in the face of rigorous physical standards. Therefore, mental health is not just an adjunct but a fundamental component of achieving and maintaining peak physical fitness in bodybuilding.

Understanding The Mindset Of A Bodybuilder

The mindset of a bodybuilder is characterized by a unique blend of discipline, resilience, and a relentless pursuit of perfection. Renowned bodybuilder and seven-time Mr. Olympia, Arnold Schwarzenegger, once reflected, "The mind is the limit. As long as the mind can envision the fact that you can do something, you can do it" (Schwarzenegger, 1977). This statement encapsulates the mental framework prevalent among successful bodybuilders. They possess an extraordinary ability to visualize success and have an unwavering belief in their capability to achieve their physical goals.

Bodybuilders often demonstrate an exceptional level of discipline, not just in their rigorous training routines but also in their strict dietary practices. This discipline extends beyond the gym; it is a lifestyle commitment. The psychological resilience required to persistently adhere to such a demanding regimen is substantial. Bodybuilders need to maintain focus and motivation, often for extended periods, to see tangible results. This requirement for sustained mental effort is as challenging as the physical demands of the sport.

The bodybuilder's mindset also involves coping with pain and discomfort, pushing the body beyond its perceived limits, and continually striving for improvement. This requires a high level of mental toughness, a trait emphasized by sports psychologists as critical for success in any sport (Weinberg & Gould, 2015). Bodybuilders must also manage the psychological aspects of competing, which involves dealing with pressure, handling both victory and defeat, and constantly comparing oneself against others.

Common Psychological Challenges Faced By Bodybuilders

Bodybuilders face several psychological challenges that can impact their training and performance. One of the primary challenges is maintaining sustained motivation, especially given the long periods required to see physical changes. As sports psychologist Dr. Jim Taylor notes, "Motivation in sports is so important because you must be willing to work hard in the face of fatigue, boredom, pain, and the desire to do other things" (Taylor, 2009). This challenge is particularly acute in bodybuilding, where the repetitive nature of training and the slow rate of visible progress can lead to motivation fluctuations.

Another significant challenge is dealing with the pressure of competition. Bodybuilders often experience stress and anxiety before and during competitions, which can affect their performance. The fear of not meeting personal or public expectations can be overwhelming. The Journal of Strength and Conditioning Research highlights the impact of psychological stress on athletes, showing that it can lead to decreased performance and increased risk of injury (Smith, 2003).

Body image issues also pose a psychological challenge. Bodybuilders, by the nature of their sport, focus intensively on their physical appearance. This intense focus can sometimes lead to negative body image or disorders like muscle dysmorphia, where individuals have a distorted perception of their body. According to a study published in Psychology of Sport and Exercise, such disorders are more prevalent in sports that emphasize appearance, size, and symmetry, like bodybuilding (Grieve, 2007).

Lastly, the discipline required for strict dieting and the mental resilience needed to endure physical pain during intense workouts are significant psychological hurdles. These aspects of bodybuilding require a level of mental toughness and self-control that can be mentally exhausting over time.

The common psychological challenges faced by bodybuilders are multifaceted, ranging from maintaining motivation and managing competition stress to dealing with body image issues and the mental demands of diet and exercise discipline. These challenges require bodybuilders to develop strong mental coping strategies to succeed in their sport.

The Role Of Mental Health In Physical Fitness

Mental health plays a crucial role in physical fitness, a relationship that is particularly evident in disciplines like bodybuilding. According to Dr. Michael Sachs, a professor of Kinesiology at Temple University, "The mind is the athlete; the body is simply the means it uses" (Sachs, 2004). This statement underscores the idea that mental health is foundational to physical performance. Mental well-being influences motivation, focus, and the ability to persist through challenging training routines.

Research in the field of sport psychology consistently shows that mental health issues can adversely affect physical performance. For example, a study published in the Journal of Applied Sport Psychology found that psychological stress can negatively impact an athlete's concentration, confidence, and ultimately their performance (Gould & Dieffenbach, 2002). In bodybuilding, where precision, focus, and long-term commitment are essential, mental health issues can hinder a bodybuilder's ability to maintain consistent training and dietary regimens.

Furthermore, positive mental health contributes to better recovery processes. A study in the Journal of Sport and Exercise Psychology demonstrated that athletes with higher levels of mental well-being experienced more efficient recovery from physical exertion (Kenttä & Hassmén, 1998). For bodybuilders, recovery is as crucial as the workouts themselves, as it allows for muscle repair and growth.

Mental health also affects an individual's resilience and ability to handle the physical demands and occasional setbacks in training. Bodybuilders, like all athletes, encounter periods of plateau, injury, or fatigue. A robust mental state helps to navigate these challenges without losing sight of long-term goals.

Techniques For Developing Mental Toughness

Developing mental toughness is essential for athletes, especially in disciplines like bodybuilding where the mental challenges are as demanding as the physical ones. According to sports psychologist Dr. Jim Afremow, "Mental toughness is about how effectively you handle pressure, not how much you can endure" (Afremow, 2015). This perspective emphasizes the importance of managing stress and maintaining focus under pressure.

One effective technique for developing mental toughness is goal setting. Setting specific, measurable, attainable, relevant, and time-bound (SMART) goals helps athletes stay focused and motivated. A study in the Journal of Applied Sport Psychology illustrates that goal setting enhances athletes' motivation and performance (Weinberg, 1994).

Visualization is another powerful tool. It involves mentally rehearsing successful performances and imagining overcoming obstacles. Dr. Afremow states, "Seeing in your mind's eye the performance you want to reproduce or the obstacle you want to overcome prepares you mentally to execute successfully" (Afremow, 2015). Visualization has been shown to improve concentration, confidence, and performance.

Additionally, practicing mindfulness and meditation can significantly enhance mental toughness. These practices help in maintaining focus, managing stress, and staying present during training and competition. A study in the journal Mindfulness found that mindfulness training improved athletes' attention, awareness, and resilience (Gardner & Moore, 2004).

Graded exposure to stress is also a technique used to build mental toughness. This involves gradually exposing oneself to the stressors of competition in a controlled way, thereby increasing tolerance and reducing anxiety over time. Sports psychologist Dr. Andrea Firth-Clark explains, "By gradually increasing the exposure to pressure situations, athletes can desensitize themselves to the stress and learn to perform under it" (Firth-Clark, 2012).

In summary, techniques such as goal setting, visualization, mindfulness, and graded exposure to stress are effective in developing the mental toughness required for high-level athletic performance, particularly in sports like bodybuilding. These techniques help athletes manage pressure, stay focused, and maintain resilience, which are key components of mental toughness.

Strategies For Overcoming Setbacks And Failures

Overcoming setbacks and failures is a critical aspect of athletic training, particularly in disciplines like bodybuilding where progress can be slow and demanding. Sports psychologist Dr. Jim Taylor emphasizes that "Setbacks are a natural part of the growth process because if you're extending yourself to reach your upper limits, you're bound to encounter obstacles" (Taylor, 2011). Recognizing setbacks as opportunities for growth rather than insurmountable barriers is a fundamental strategy.

One effective strategy for overcoming setbacks is reframing how these events are perceived. Instead of viewing them as failures, athletes can see them as learning experiences. A study in the Journal of Applied Sport Psychology discusses the concept of cognitive restructuring, which involves changing negative thought patterns about setbacks into more positive, constructive ones (Jones, 2002).

Another strategy is maintaining a strong support network. The presence of supportive coaches, trainers, and peers can provide the necessary encouragement and perspective during challenging times. Research in sports psychology has shown that social support can significantly improve an athlete's ability to deal with stress and setbacks (Rees, 2007).

Setting short-term, achievable goals following a setback is also beneficial. This approach helps in maintaining motivation and provides a clear roadmap for recovery and progress. Dr. Taylor advises, "Short-term goals give you immediate, manageable goals that can provide a sense of accomplishment" (Taylor, 2011).

Additionally, practicing resilience-building techniques like mindfulness and mental imagery can aid in emotional and mental recovery. These techniques help in managing negative emotions and maintaining focus on future goals. A study in the International Journal of Sports Science & Coaching found that mental training, including relaxation techniques and mental imagery, improved athletes' ability to bounce back from setbacks (Fletcher & Sarkar, 2012).

Strategies such as cognitive restructuring, maintaining a support network, setting short-term goals, and practicing resilience-building techniques are effective in helping athletes overcome setbacks and failures. These strategies enable athletes to view challenges as opportunities for learning and growth, which is essential for long-term success in sports like bodybuilding.

The Power Of A Positive Mindset In Training

The power of a positive mindset in training is a well-established concept in sports psychology, especially pertinent in disciplines like bodybuilding where mental tenacity is as critical as physical strength. Dr. Carol Dweck's research on mindset underscores this, revealing that individuals with a growth mindset – those who believe abilities can be developed – are more resilient and successful in their pursuits (Dweck, 2006). In the context of bodybuilding, a positive mindset can significantly influence an athlete's ability to persist through grueling training schedules and setbacks.

Athletes with a positive mindset tend to view challenges as opportunities for growth rather than insurmountable obstacles. They are more likely to maintain motivation and commitment even in the face of adversity. A study in the Journal of Applied Sport Psychology showed that athletes with a positive attitude displayed greater persistence, better performance, and higher levels of satisfaction (Vealey, 2007).

Furthermore, a positive mindset aids in stress management and recovery. Optimism has been linked to lower stress levels and better coping strategies. The Journal of Sport & Exercise Psychology published findings indicating that athletes with positive attitudes recovered more quickly from injuries and were better at managing the psychological stress of recovery (Podlog & Eklund, 2007).

Additionally, a positive mindset can enhance focus and concentration during training. Athletes who maintain a positive attitude are less likely to be distracted by negative thoughts, enabling them to concentrate more effectively on their training goals. Dr. Dweck's research also suggests that a growth mindset fosters a love of learning and a resilience that is essential for great accomplishment (Dweck, 2006).

Cultivating a positive mindset in training offers numerous benefits for bodybuilders. It fosters resilience, enhances focus, aids in stress management, and facilitates recovery, contributing significantly to both physical and mental performance in the sport.

Exploring Sources Of Motivation In Bodybuilding

In bodybuilding, motivation is a multifaceted concept with varied sources. Dr. Jim Taylor, an authority in sports psychology, asserts that motivation in sports comes from both internal and external sources (Taylor, 2009). Internally, bodybuilders often draw motivation from personal goals, such as improving health, enhancing physical appearance, or achieving a sense of accomplishment. These intrinsic motivators are crucial for long-term commitment to the sport, as they are rooted in personal satisfaction and self-fulfillment.

Externally, bodybuilders may find motivation in the desire for recognition, competition success, or social validation. Competing in bodybuilding events, receiving feedback from judges and peers, and gaining social recognition can serve as powerful motivational drivers. A study in the Journal of Sports Sciences found that external rewards and recognition can significantly enhance an athlete's motivation (Ryan & Deci, 2000).

The role of community and social support in bodybuilding also serves as a source of motivation. Being part of a bodybuilding community provides a sense of belonging and shared purpose. This communal aspect can motivate athletes to adhere to their training and diet regimes more strictly. Research in the International Journal of Sport and Exercise Psychology highlights the positive impact of social support on athletes' motivation (Smith, 2003).

Setting and achieving goals is another critical source of motivation in bodybuilding. Goal setting helps bodybuilders maintain focus and direction in their training. Achieving these goals, whether they are related to lifting weights, body composition, or performance in competitions, provides a sense of progress and accomplishment. According to a study in the Journal of Applied Sport Psychology, goal setting is linked to increased motivation and improved performance in sports (Locke & Latham, 2002).

Sources of motivation in bodybuilding are diverse, encompassing both intrinsic factors like personal satisfaction and health, and extrinsic factors such as recognition, community support, and goal achievement. Understanding and leveraging these motivational sources is essential for success and longevity in the sport.

Long-Term Goal Setting And Maintaining Focus

In the context of bodybuilding, long-term goal setting and maintaining focus are essential for success. Dr. Edwin Locke's seminal research on goal-setting theory highlights the effectiveness of setting specific and challenging goals in enhancing performance (Locke & Latham, 2002). For bodybuilders, long-term goals often revolve around achieving certain physical standards, such as muscle mass, body fat percentage, or lifting targets. These goals provide a clear direction and purpose, essential for sustained effort over time.

Maintaining focus over the long term, especially in a sport as demanding as bodybuilding, requires more than just setting goals. It involves a continuous commitment to the training process and an unwavering dedication to dietary regimens. Sports psychologist Dr. Jim Taylor emphasizes the importance of focus in athletic success, stating, "Focus is so important because it's the gateway to all thinking: perception, memory, learning, reasoning, problem-solving, and decision making" (Taylor, 2009). In bodybuilding, this focus is critical not only in executing exercises but also in adhering to the strategic planning of training cycles and nutrition.

To maintain focus, bodybuilders often utilize techniques such as visualization, where they imagine themselves achieving their goals, and self-talk, to reinforce their commitment and maintain a positive mindset. A study in the Journal of Applied Sport Psychology demonstrated that these mental training techniques could significantly improve athletes' focus and performance (Gardner & Moore, 2004).

Additionally, monitoring progress towards long-term goals is vital. This can be achieved through regular assessments of physical changes, tracking workout performance, and periodically revisiting and adjusting goals as necessary. This process of monitoring and evaluation helps bodybuilders stay aligned with their long-term objectives, making necessary adjustments to training and nutrition to optimize progress.

In summary, long-term goal setting in bodybuilding is a detailed and strategic process that goes beyond mere aspiration. It requires a combination of specific, challenging goals, continuous focus, and regular progress monitoring. These elements are crucial in maintaining motivation and ensuring sustained progress in the demanding world of bodybuilding.

Overcoming Periods Of Low Motivation

Overcoming periods of low motivation is a common challenge in bodybuilding, where the rigorous demands of training and diet can sometimes lead to mental fatigue and a decrease in motivation. Sports psychologist Dr. Jim Taylor describes low motivation as a significant barrier to athletic success and emphasizes the importance of identifying and addressing its underlying causes (Taylor, 2009). In bodybuilding, periods of low motivation can stem from various factors, including burnout, plateaued progress, or a lack of variation in training routines.

One effective strategy for overcoming these periods is setting short-term, achievable goals. These can provide immediate motivation boosts and a sense of accomplishment. According to a study in the Journal of Clinical Psychology, short-term goals can act as stepping stones to larger objectives, helping maintain motivation over longer periods.

Another approach is varying the training regimen. This not only helps in preventing physical plateau but also keeps the training process engaging and mentally stimulating. Sports science research indicates that variety in training can prevent boredom and sustain athletes' interest and motivation.

Reconnecting with the intrinsic reasons for pursuing bodybuilding can also reignite motivation. Whether it's for personal health, the joy of improving, or the satisfaction of meeting personal challenges, reminding oneself of these core motivations can provide a renewed sense of purpose.

Additionally, seeking social support from fellow bodybuilders, coaches, or mentors can provide encouragement and perspective during low motivation periods. The Journal of Sport & Exercise Psychology published findings showing the positive impact of social support on athletes' motivation and overall well-being (Smith, 2003).

Identifying And Overcoming Self-Doubt

Identifying and overcoming self-doubt is a crucial psychological aspect in bodybuilding, a sport where confidence can significantly influence performance. Self-doubt often arises from internal negative self-talk or comparisons with others, leading to decreased motivation and performance. Sports psychologist Dr. Jim Afremow notes, "Self-doubt is the number one killer of athletes' dreams" (Afremow, 2015). In bodybuilding, where the focus on physical perfection is intense, self-doubt can be particularly debilitating.

The first step in overcoming self-doubt is identifying its sources, which may include past failures, unrealistic expectations, or negative feedback. Recognizing these triggers allows bodybuilders to address them directly. Cognitive-behavioral strategies, such as challenging negative thoughts and replacing them with more positive, constructive ones, have been shown to be effective. A study in the Journal of Applied Sport Psychology demonstrates the efficacy of cognitive restructuring in reducing self-doubt and enhancing performance (Beck, 1979).

Building a strong support system is also crucial in overcoming self-doubt. Coaches, trainers, and fellow athletes can provide encouragement, feedback, and a more objective perspective on an athlete's abilities and progress. The Journal of Sport Behavior published findings indicating the positive impact of social support on reducing athletes' self-doubt (Udry, 1997).

Setting realistic and achievable goals can further help in building confidence and reducing self-doubt. Achieving these smaller goals provides a sense of progress and accomplishment, bolstering self-esteem and belief in one's capabilities. Research in the Journal of Sport and Exercise Psychology highlights the importance of goal-setting in enhancing athletes' self-confidence (Bandura, 1997).

Finally, practicing self-compassion and mindfulness can be beneficial. These practices encourage a non-judgmental acceptance of one's abilities and limitations, reducing the tendency to engage in negative self-comparisons. A study in Psychology of Sport and Exercise found that athletes who practiced mindfulness and self-compassion experienced lower levels of self-doubt (Gardner & Moore, 2004).

In summary, overcoming self-doubt in bodybuilding involves identifying its sources, employing cognitive-behavioral strategies, building a supportive network, setting realistic goals, and practicing self-compassion and mindfulness. These strategies collectively help in building mental resilience and confidence, essential for success in bodybuilding.

Building A Strong Sense Of Self-Confidence

Building a strong sense of self-confidence is fundamental in bodybuilding, where mental strength significantly impacts physical performance. According to sports psychologist Dr. Jim Taylor, "Confidence is the single most important mental factor in sports" (Taylor, 2009). Confidence in bodybuilding stems from a belief in one's abilities and the assurance that one can meet the challenges of training and competition.

Developing self-confidence often begins with consistent and successful training experiences. As bodybuilders achieve their training goals, their belief in their abilities strengthens. A study in the Journal of Applied Sport Psychology supports this, showing that mastery experiences, or successes in training, are the most robust source of self-confidence for athletes (Vealey, 1986).

Positive self-talk is another critical tool in building self-confidence. Replacing negative or self-doubting thoughts with affirmations and positive statements can change the mental narrative. Research in the field of sports psychology has shown that positive self-talk can enhance performance and confidence (Hardy, 1997).

Visualization techniques can also contribute to building self-confidence. By mentally rehearsing successful training sessions or visualizing achievement in competitions, bodybuilders can strengthen their mental readiness and self-belief. The International Journal of Sport and Exercise Psychology published findings indicating that visualization enhances athletes' confidence and performance (Cumming & Hall, 2002).

Moreover, setting and achieving short-term, realistic goals is essential in building self-confidence. Achieving these goals provides tangible evidence of progress, reinforcing the belief in one's capabilities. This approach aligns with Dr. Albert Bandura's self-efficacy theory, which posits that successful experiences boost self-efficacy, a key component of confidence (Bandura, 1977).

Building a strong sense of self-confidence in bodybuilding involves achieving success in training, engaging in positive self-talk, practicing visualization, and setting and achieving realistic goals. These strategies help in fostering a robust belief in one's abilities, essential for success in the highly competitive and physically demanding world of bodybuilding.

Role Of Self-Talk And Affirmations In Building Mental Strength

The role of self-talk and affirmations in building mental strength is pivotal in sports, particularly in bodybuilding where mental resilience is as essential as physical strength. Self-talk, the internal dialogue an individual has with themselves, can significantly impact performance.

Sports psychologist Dr. Antonis Hatzigeorgiadis states, "Self-talk is a key psychological tool for enhancing performance. It's about reinforcing confidence and success in athletes" (Hatzigeorgiadis, 2011). In bodybuilding, positive self-talk can help athletes overcome doubts, maintain focus during training, and enhance performance.

Affirmations, or positive statements about oneself and one's abilities, are another powerful tool. By affirming their strengths and capabilities, bodybuilders can cultivate a mindset conducive to success. A study in the Journal of Sports Sciences found that affirmations can boost athletes' self-confidence and reduce performance anxiety .

The effectiveness of self-talk and affirmations in building mental strength lies in their ability to influence mindset and attitude. Negative self-talk can lead to self-doubt and reduced performance, while positive self-talk and affirmations can foster a positive attitude, resilience, and perseverance. This psychological aspect is crucial in bodybuilding, where athletes face intense physical demands and need to maintain motivation and confidence over extended periods.

Additionally, self-talk and affirmations can aid in goal setting and visualization, integral components of mental training in bodybuilding. Repeating affirmations related to specific goals can help in maintaining focus on these objectives, while positive self-talk during training can enhance concentration and effort.

Self-talk and affirmations play a critical role in building mental strength in bodybuilding. They contribute to a positive mental state, reinforce confidence and resilience, and are essential tools for overcoming the psychological challenges of the sport.

Understanding Steroids And Their Role In Bodybuilding

Steroids, synthetic variants of the male sex hormone testosterone, play a controversial role in bodybuilding. Their primary function is to promote muscle growth and enhance physical performance, which is why they are appealing in the competitive bodybuilding world. However, the use of anabolic-androgenic steroids (AAS) in sports is banned by major organizations due to their potential health risks and unfair advantage in performance. Despite this, the prevalence of steroid use in bodybuilding remains a significant issue.

The appeal of steroids in bodybuilding stems from their ability to increase muscle mass and reduce body fat more quickly than through natural training. According to a study published in Sports Medicine, steroids can significantly increase lean muscle mass in comparison to non-users (Hartgens & Kuipers, 2004). They also improve recovery time, allowing athletes to train harder and more frequently.

However, the use of steroids is associated with serious health risks, including liver damage, cardiovascular issues, hormonal imbalances, and psychological effects like aggression and depression. The Journal of Internal Medicine published a study highlighting these risks, emphasizing the potential long-term health consequences of steroid use (Pope et al., 2014).

The ethical dilemma in bodybuilding concerning steroid use revolves around fairness and health. While some argue for the freedom of choice in using steroids, others point to the health risks and the unfair advantage they provide in competitions. This ethical debate is ongoing in the bodybuilding community.

Steroids play a complex role in bodybuilding. They offer significant benefits in muscle growth and recovery but pose serious health risks and ethical concerns. The debate over their use highlights the tension between the desire for competitive success and the importance of health and fair play in sports.

Psychological Effects Of Steroid Use

The psychological effects of steroid use, particularly in the context of bodybuilding, are significant and multifaceted. Anabolic-androgenic steroids (AAS), while enhancing physical performance and muscle mass, can also lead to a range of psychological effects. According to research published in the Journal of Sports Science and Medicine, users may experience mood swings, increased aggressiveness, and manic-like symptoms, often referred to as "roid rage" (Trenton & Currier, 2005).

Additionally, AAS use is associated with increased risk of psychological dependence. A study in Drug and Alcohol Dependence found that some steroid users exhibit addictive behaviors, continuing use despite negative consequences (Kanayama et al., 2009). This dependency can stem from the desire to maintain enhanced physical appearance and performance, and the withdrawal symptoms upon cessation can include depression and lethargy.

Steroid use also impacts self-esteem and body image. The International Journal of Sports Medicine published findings showing that long-term steroid use can lead to body dysmorphic disorders, particularly muscle dysmorphia, characterized by a distorted self-image and obsessive concern with muscularity (Pope et al., 2000).

Furthermore, steroid use can exacerbate underlying mental health issues. Individuals with pre-existing mental health conditions may experience heightened symptoms due to the hormonal imbalances caused by steroids. The American Journal of Psychiatry notes that steroid users with no prior history of mental illness have exhibited psychiatric symptoms ranging from mood disorders to psychotic episodes (Pope & Katz, 1994).

The psychological effects of steroid use in bodybuilding are profound, ranging from mood disturbances and aggressive behavior to dependency, body image disorders, and exacerbation of mental health conditions. These effects underscore the potential mental health risks associated with steroid use.

Dilemma Of Steroids In Competitive Bodybuilding

The use of anabolic-androgenic steroids (AAS) in competitive bodybuilding presents a significant ethical dilemma. While steroids can enhance muscle mass and physical performance, their use is banned in professional sports due to health risks and the unfair advantage they provide. This ban is upheld by major sports organizations, including the International Olympic Committee (IOC) and the World Anti-Doping Agency (WADA). The ethical debate centers on the integrity of the sport, athletes' health, and the message it sends to society.

Advocates against steroid use argue that it undermines the spirit of fair competition, giving users an unnatural advantage over those who choose to stay natural. Moreover, the health risks associated with steroid use, including cardiovascular issues, liver damage, and psychological effects, raise concerns about the long-term well-being of athletes (Hartgens & Kuipers, 2004, Sports Medicine).

On the other hand, some argue for the autonomy of athletes in making choices about their bodies, suggesting that informed adults should be allowed to use steroids if they accept the associated risks. This perspective also points to the challenge of effectively policing steroid use, given the availability of sophisticated masking agents and the continuous development of new performance-enhancing substances.

The ethical dilemma is further complicated by the fact that bodybuilding, unlike many other sports, places a premium on physical appearance and muscle size, factors directly influenced by steroid use. This can create pressure on athletes to use steroids to remain competitive.

The Impact Of Steroids On Mental Wellness

The impact of anabolic-androgenic steroids (AAS) on mental wellness is a critical concern, particularly in the context of sports like bodybuilding. While steroids are known for their physical performance-enhancing effects, their psychological impact can be profound and detrimental. Research in the field of sports medicine has indicated that steroid use can lead to a range of mental health issues. A study published in the journal "Addiction" found that steroid users are more likely to experience mood disorders, including mania and depression (Pope & Katz, 1994).

Users often report feelings of irritability, aggression, and heightened anxiety, commonly referred to as "roid rage." This term has been associated with significant changes in mood and behavior among steroid users, as documented in the "Journal of Clinical Psychiatry" (Trenton & Currier, 2005). Furthermore, dependence on steroids can develop, leading to withdrawal symptoms like depression and lethargy when usage is reduced or stopped, as discussed in the "Journal of Pharmacology and Pharmacotherapeutics" (Kanayama et al., 2010).

Steroid use has also been linked to impaired judgment and increased risk-taking behavior, which can have serious implications for mental health. The "Journal of Forensic Sciences" highlighted cases where steroid use was a contributing factor in criminal behavior, underscoring its potential impact on mental stability and decision-making (Thiblin et al., 2000).

These psychological effects, coupled with the physical health risks, make steroid use a significant concern for mental wellness, especially in sports where its use is prevalent. The mental health risks associated with steroids underscore the need for awareness and education about the consequences of their use.

Recognizing And Addressing Dependency Issues

Recognizing and addressing dependency issues, particularly in the context of anabolic-androgenic steroid (AAS) use in bodybuilding, is crucial. Dependency on steroids can develop both psychologically and physically. According to the National Institute on Drug Abuse, individuals using steroids can develop a dependence syndrome, leading to withdrawal symptoms such as depression, fatigue, and irritability when steroid use is discontinued (NIDA, 2020).

The process of recognizing dependency involves being aware of signs such as an uncontrollable desire to use steroids despite knowledge of adverse effects, significant time spent in obtaining and using steroids, and continued use despite physical or psychological problems. A study in the Journal of Psychoactive Drugs reported that individuals with steroid dependency often experience a loss of control over their steroid use and spend excessive amounts of time and money obtaining the drugs (Kanayama et al., 2009).

Addressing these issues requires a multifaceted approach. First, education about the risks of steroid use and its potential for dependency is essential. Health professionals and trainers should inform athletes about the dangers of steroids and provide guidance on natural bodybuilding methods.

For those struggling with dependency, psychological interventions can be effective. Cognitive-behavioral therapy (CBT) has been shown to be beneficial in treating substance use disorders, including steroid dependency. This approach helps individuals change their thought patterns and behaviors related to steroid use (Bates & McVeigh, 2016, Journal of Substance Use).

Additionally, support groups can provide a community for those dealing with steroid dependency, offering a space to share experiences and coping strategies. Medical intervention may also be necessary in some cases, particularly when dealing with withdrawal symptoms.

Managing Stress And Anxiety In Competitions

Managing stress and anxiety in competitions is a critical aspect of mental preparation for bodybuilders. The high-pressure environment of competitive bodybuilding can elicit significant stress and anxiety, which can negatively impact performance. Sports psychologist Dr. Kate Hays states, "The ability to manage anxiety is an integral part of athletic competition" (Hays, 2009). In bodybuilding, where competitors are judged on their physique and presentation, the psychological pressure can be particularly intense.

Effective management of competition-related stress and anxiety often involves techniques such as deep breathing, meditation, and visualization. These practices can help athletes maintain calm and focus in the face of competition pressures. Research in the Journal of Applied Sport Psychology demonstrates that relaxation and mental imagery exercises can significantly reduce anxiety and improve performance in athletes.

Additionally, developing a consistent pre-competition routine can help in managing stress. This routine can include specific warm-up exercises, mental rehearsal, and positive self-talk. A study in the International Journal of Sports Science & Coaching found that routines help athletes feel more in control and less anxious during competitions.

Another strategy is to focus on the process rather than the outcome. Concentrating on executing well-practiced routines and maintaining optimal form can divert attention away from anxiety about the results. The Journal of Sports Sciences published findings that process-focused strategies are associated with lower anxiety levels and better performance (Beilock & Gray, 2007).

In conclusion, managing stress and anxiety in bodybuilding competitions involves a combination of relaxation techniques, consistent pre-competition routines, and a process-focused approach. These strategies are crucial for bodybuilders to perform their best under the high-pressure conditions of competitive events.

Techniques For Staying Calm And Focused Under Pressure

Staying calm and focused under pressure, especially in competitive sports like bodybuilding, is essential for optimal performance. Sports psychologist Dr. Jim Afremow emphasizes the importance of mental toughness in high-pressure situations, stating, "The heart of mental toughness is the ability to stay calm and focused under pressure" (Afremow, 2015). Several techniques are employed by athletes to maintain composure and concentration during critical moments.

Breathing exercises are a fundamental technique for managing stress and maintaining calm. Controlled breathing helps lower the heart rate and reduce anxiety, allowing for better focus. A study in the Journal of Sports Science & Medicine found that diaphragmatic breathing significantly decreases physiological markers of stress in athletes (Jones, 2018).

Another effective technique is visualization or mental rehearsal. Athletes mentally simulate their performance, focusing on successful execution and positive outcomes. This practice enhances focus and preparedness. Research published in the Journal of Applied Sport Psychology demonstrates that visualization improves concentration and performance in competitive sports .

Mindfulness and meditation are also widely used to enhance focus and reduce stress. These practices involve being present in the moment and acknowledging thoughts and feelings without judgment. A study in the

International Journal of Sports Psychology found that mindfulness meditation improves athletes' focus and reduces performance anxiety.

Positive self-talk is another key technique for staying calm and focused. Replacing negative thoughts with positive affirmations can boost confidence and focus. According to the Journal of Sports Sciences, positive self-talk is linked to improved performance and focus in athletes (Hardy et al., 2009).

In summary, techniques such as breathing exercises, visualization, mindfulness, and positive self-talk are crucial for bodybuilders and athletes to stay calm and focused under pressure. These practices enable them to manage stress, maintain concentration, and perform at their best during competitions.

Balancing Competition With Personal Life And Mental Health

Balancing competition with personal life and mental health is a significant challenge in bodybuilding, a sport that demands intense physical and mental commitment. Dr. Jim Afremow, a sports psychologist, notes the importance of this balance: "Athletes need to find a balance between their sport and personal life to maintain overall well-being" (Afremow, 2015). The all-consuming nature of bodybuilding, with its rigorous training and strict dietary regimes, can often lead to neglect of personal relationships and mental health.

To achieve this balance, setting boundaries is crucial. Athletes must allocate specific times for training, rest, and personal activities, ensuring that one aspect of their life does not disproportionately consume their time and energy. A study in the Journal of Applied Sport Psychology highlights the importance of time management skills in maintaining life balance for athletes.

Prioritizing mental health is also essential. Engaging in regular mental health practices such as mindfulness, meditation, and psychological counseling can help maintain mental well-being. Research in the International Journal of Sports Science & Coaching found that mental health interventions improve athletes' overall well-being and performance.

Maintaining a strong support network, including family, friends, and coaches, can provide emotional support and perspective. This network can remind athletes of their life outside of the sport, helping them stay grounded. The Journal of Sport and Exercise Psychology published findings indicating the positive impact of social support on athletes' mental health and life satisfaction.

Incorporating Mindfulness And Meditation Into Training

Incorporating mindfulness and meditation into training has become increasingly recognized for its benefits in sports, including bodybuilding. Mindfulness involves being present and fully engaged in the moment without judgment, while meditation is a practice of focus and relaxation. Dr. Jon Kabat-Zinn, a pioneer in mindfulness research, asserts that these practices can significantly reduce stress and improve performance (Kabat-Zinn, 2003).

In bodybuilding, mindfulness and meditation can enhance focus during training, allowing athletes to concentrate fully on their exercises and form. A study in the Journal of Health Psychology found that mindfulness training improved athletes' concentration and reduced performance anxiety (Moore, 2009).

Meditation, particularly techniques focusing on breathing and relaxation, can aid in recovery and stress management. The International Journal of Sports Medicine published research showing that meditation can lower cortisol levels, a hormone associated with stress, and enhance overall well-being (Solberg et al., 2000).

Incorporating these practices into training routines can involve short meditation sessions before or after workouts, or integrating mindful breathing exercises during rest periods. Athletes might also engage in regular mindfulness meditation sessions separate from their physical training.

The benefits of mindfulness and meditation in bodybuilding extend beyond physical performance. They contribute to mental health by reducing stress, preventing burnout, and promoting a balanced approach to training. This holistic approach to athlete development is increasingly seen as essential in the competitive world of bodybuilding.

The Role Of Mental Training In Physical Performance

The role of mental training in enhancing physical performance is crucial, particularly in sports like bodybuilding where both physical and mental strength are key. Dr. Jim Afremow, a noted sports psychologist, emphasizes the importance of mental training, stating, "Mental training is as important as physical training in sports" (Afremow, 2015). Mental training techniques, including visualization, goal setting, and positive self-talk, can significantly impact an athlete's performance.

Visualization, or mental rehearsal, involves athletes imagining themselves executing their physical routines successfully. This technique not only prepares them mentally for the task at hand but also enhances their confidence and focus. Research in the Journal of Applied Sport Psychology shows that visualization can improve athletic performance by enhancing motivation and reducing anxiety .

Goal setting is another vital aspect of mental training. Setting specific, measurable, achievable, relevant, and time-bound (SMART) goals helps athletes maintain focus and direction in their training. According to a study in the Journal of Sport and Exercise Psychology, goal setting is linked to higher motivation and better performance in sports (Locke & Latham, 2002).

Positive self-talk, the practice of replacing negative thoughts with positive affirmations, can boost an athlete's confidence and resilience. Research in the Journal of Sports Sciences found that positive self-talk enhances performance by increasing effort and concentration .

Techniques For Mental Relaxation And Recovery

In the demanding realm of bodybuilding, techniques for mental relaxation and recovery are essential. These practices help mitigate the stress of intense training and competition, supporting overall well-being and performance. Sports psychologist Dr. Jim Afremow asserts the importance of mental recovery, stating, "Relaxation and recovery are as important as training" (Afremow, 2015). Effective techniques for mental relaxation and recovery include progressive muscle relaxation, guided imagery, and breathing exercises.

Progressive muscle relaxation involves systematically tensing and then relaxing different muscle groups. This technique helps in reducing physical tension, which is often linked to mental stress. A study in the Journal of Behavioral Therapy and Experimental Psychiatry demonstrated that progressive muscle relaxation can significantly decrease anxiety levels in athletes.

Guided imagery, a form of visualization, involves imagining a peaceful and relaxing scene or situation. This technique not only aids in mental relaxation but also enhances mood and focus. Research in the Journal of Applied Sport Psychology found that guided imagery could reduce stress and improve athletes' coping skills.

Breathing exercises, particularly diaphragmatic breathing, are another effective method for promoting mental relaxation. By focusing on slow, deep breaths, athletes can activate their parasympathetic nervous system, reducing the physiological symptoms of stress. The International Journal of Yoga published findings showing that diaphragmatic breathing can decrease cortisol levels, a stress hormone, thereby promoting relaxation.

Incorporating these mental relaxation and recovery techniques into a regular training regimen can significantly benefit bodybuilders, helping them manage stress, recover from the mental demands of training, and maintain peak performance.

Integrating Mental Health Practices Into Daily Routines

Integrating mental health practices into daily routines is vital for athletes, particularly in bodybuilding, where the mental strain of continuous training and dieting can be as taxing as the physical demands. Dr. Jim Afremow, a sports psychologist, emphasizes the significance of mental health in athletic performance, stating, "Mental health is not just the absence of problems; it's the ability to manage life effectively" (Afremow, 2015). Key mental health practices include mindfulness, positive self-talk, and regular mental health check-ins.

Mindfulness, the practice of being present and fully engaged in the current moment, can be integrated into daily routines. It can be practiced during training, eating, or rest periods. A study in the Journal of Clinical Psychology found that mindfulness improves focus, reduces stress, and enhances emotional regulation (Gardner & Moore, 2012).

Positive self-talk, involving the use of affirmative and encouraging dialogue with oneself, is another beneficial practice. This can be particularly effective during training sessions or in preparation for competitions. The Journal of Sports Sciences reports that positive self-talk improves self-confidence and reduces negative emotions .

Regular mental health check-ins, where athletes assess their mental state and address any emerging issues, are also important. This could involve self-reflection or discussions with coaches, psychologists, or peers. A study in the Journal of Applied Sport Psychology highlights the benefits of mental health monitoring in preventing burnout and maintaining motivation.

Incorporating these mental health practices into daily routines helps bodybuilders maintain psychological well-being, which is crucial for sustaining high-level performance in the sport.

The Importance Of Rest, Nutrition, And Life Outside The Gym

In the world of bodybuilding, the importance of rest, nutrition, and life outside the gym is paramount for both physical and mental well-being. Dr. John Berardi, a nutrition expert, underscores the significance of these aspects, noting, "Recovery, nutrition, and life balance are as important as the training itself" (Berardi, 2007). Adequate rest is essential for muscle recovery and growth, and neglecting it can lead to overtraining syndrome, characterized by fatigue and decreased performance. The Journal of Sports Sciences reports that proper rest is crucial for physiological and psychological recovery in athletes (Halson, 2008).

Nutrition plays a critical role in bodybuilding, providing the energy and nutrients needed for training and recovery. A balanced diet that includes adequate protein, carbohydrates, fats, and micronutrients is essential. The International Journal of Sport Nutrition and Exercise Metabolism emphasizes that appropriate nutritional strategies enhance training outcomes and overall health in athletes (Kerksick et al., 2008).

Equally important is maintaining a life outside the gym. Engaging in social activities, hobbies, and other interests can prevent burnout and contribute to a more balanced lifestyle. A study in the Journal of Sport and Exercise Psychology found that athletes with a well-rounded life outside of their sport experienced lower stress levels and higher life satisfaction.

Strategies For A Sustainable And Healthy Bodybuilding Career

For a sustainable and healthy bodybuilding career, adopting specific strategies is essential. According to Dr. Nicholas A. Ratamess, a prominent figure in sports science, "Long-term success in bodybuilding is contingent upon a balanced approach that encompasses both physical and mental health" (Ratamess, 2015). A key strategy is periodization of training, which involves varying the training regimen to prevent overtraining and promote continuous progress. The Journal of Strength and Conditioning Research highlights that periodization helps in preventing injuries and burnout while optimizing performance .

Proper nutrition is another cornerstone of a sustainable bodybuilding career. It involves consuming a balanced diet tailored to the demands of the training cycle, ensuring adequate intake of protein, carbohydrates, fats, and essential micronutrients. The International Society of Sports Nutrition posits that a well-planned, nutrient-dense diet is essential for muscle growth, recovery, and overall health.

Additionally, integrating rest and recovery into the training schedule is crucial. This includes not only adequate sleep but also incorporating rest days and active recovery periods. Research in Sports Medicine indicates that rest is vital for physiological adaptation and injury prevention.

Mental health practices, such as mindfulness, stress management, and seeking psychological support when needed, are vital for a sustainable career. A study in the Journal of Applied Sport Psychology demonstrates that mental health interventions can enhance athletes' well-being and performance (Gardner & Moore, 2004).

Finally, maintaining a balanced life, with time for social interactions, hobbies, and personal interests outside of bodybuilding, is essential for mental well-being. The Journal of Sport and Exercise Psychology found that athletes with a balanced lifestyle exhibit lower levels of sport-related stress and higher overall life satisfaction.

Understanding Motivation in Bodybuilding

Understanding motivation in bodybuilding, particularly during the challenging bulking and cutting phases, involves exploring both internal and external drivers. Internal motivation in bodybuilding often stems from personal goals like improving health, enhancing physical appearance, or achieving a sense of accomplishment. During bulking, where the focus is on gaining muscle mass, the motivation might come from the desire to reach new personal strength records. In contrast, during cutting, where the focus shifts to reducing body fat, the motivation might be driven by the goal of achieving a leaner physique.

External motivations in bodybuilding can include factors like competition success, social recognition, or even professional opportunities. Competing in bodybuilding events and receiving feedback from judges and peers can significantly motivate athletes, especially during the cutting phase where physical aesthetics are critically evaluated.

The psychological complexities of these phases are significant. Bulking, often accompanied by increased calorie intake and intense strength training, can challenge an athlete's discipline and commitment, requiring a strong internal drive. Cutting, characterized by strict dieting and the goal of low body fat, can test an athlete's endurance and willpower, often necessitating external validation and support.

The balance between these internal and external motivations can be delicate. Relying solely on external factors like competition success can lead to unsustainable motivation, while focusing only on internal goals may not provide enough drive in the highly competitive world of bodybuilding. Therefore, understanding and harnessing both types of motivation is crucial for success and psychological well-being in both the bulking and cutting phases of bodybuilding.

Identifying Plateaus and Their Causes

Identifying plateaus and their causes in bodybuilding is crucial for continuous progress. A plateau, a period where no significant improvement in muscle gain or weight loss is observed, can have both physical and mental underpinnings. Physically, plateaus in muscle gain often result from repetitive training routines. The body adapts to the demands placed upon it, leading to diminished returns from workouts that once yielded significant gains. In terms of weight loss, plateaus may occur when the body adjusts to a lower calorie intake and metabolic rates decrease as a response, making further weight loss challenging.

Mentally, plateaus can be caused by a lack of motivation or burnout, often arising from monotonous training or diet routines. The psychological impact of not seeing expected results can lead to decreased effort or commitment to training and dietary protocols. A study in the Journal of Applied Physiology highlighted the importance of varying training stimuli to avoid plateaus.

Understanding these causes is essential for overcoming plateaus. Physically, introducing new exercises, altering intensity, and adjusting dietary intake can reinvigorate progress. Mentally, setting new goals, seeking motivational support, and ensuring adequate rest and recovery are strategies that can help push through these stagnant phases.

Mental Barriers to Progress

Mental barriers to progress in bodybuilding, particularly during the bulking and cutting phases, are significant obstacles that can impede an athlete's success. During the bulking phase, body image issues can arise as bodybuilders increase their calorie intake and gain both muscle and fat. This weight gain, although part of a strategic plan to build muscle, can sometimes negatively affect an athlete's self-esteem and body image, leading to stress and anxiety.

In the cutting phase, where the goal is to reduce body fat while maintaining muscle mass, adherence to a strict diet can be mentally challenging. The reduction in calorie intake and the need for precise nutritional management can lead to cravings, hunger, and mood swings, making it difficult to stick to the diet plan. This can be particularly mentally taxing, as it requires constant vigilance and self-control.

Both phases require significant mental resilience. The psychological pressure to adhere to strict dietary and training regimens, while simultaneously managing body image perceptions and expectations, can be overwhelming. These mental challenges can sometimes lead to unhealthy behaviors, such as overtraining or disordered eating patterns, as athletes strive to meet their goals.

To overcome these mental barriers, bodybuilders benefit from developing coping strategies such as positive self-talk, seeking support from coaches and peers, and engaging in activities outside of bodybuilding to maintain a balanced perspective. Additionally, focusing on long-term goals and the overall health benefits of bodybuilding can help maintain motivation and perspective during these challenging phases.

Revitalizing Your Training Regimen

Revitalizing a training regimen in bodybuilding, especially during the distinct phases of bulking and cutting, involves strategic adjustments to align workouts with dietary changes. During bulking, where the focus is on gaining muscle mass, training routines typically involve heavier weights with lower repetitions to maximize muscle growth. This phase often requires increased calorie and protein intake to fuel muscle repair and growth. A study in the Journal of Strength and Conditioning Research suggests that hypertrophy-focused training, combined with adequate nutrition, is most effective for muscle gain during bulking.

In the cutting phase, where the goal is to reduce body fat while retaining muscle, training may shift towards higher repetitions with moderate weights, coupled with increased cardiovascular exercises. The dietary focus in this phase is on creating a caloric deficit while maintaining sufficient protein intake to preserve muscle mass. According to research published in the International Journal of Exercise Science, incorporating a mix of resistance and aerobic training while in a caloric deficit can optimize fat loss while preserving lean body mass during cutting (Dalleck & Kjelland, 2012).

Periodization is another vital strategy for revitalizing training regimens. This involves planning variations in training intensity and volume over specific periods to prevent plateaus and continue making progress. The concept of periodization is supported by research in the Journal of Applied Sport Science Research, which indicates that it can lead to greater improvements in strength and muscle mass compared to non-periodized approaches.

Additionally, incorporating flexibility and recovery practices, such as stretching, yoga, and foam rolling, can enhance training effectiveness and reduce the risk of injury. These practices are particularly important during intense training cycles, as they help maintain muscle function and overall physical health.

Goal Setting and Re-evaluation

Goal setting and re-evaluation in bodybuilding, particularly during bulking and cutting phases, are critical for sustained progress and motivation. Setting realistic goals involves defining clear, achievable targets tailored to individual capabilities and circumstances. For bulking, goals might focus on specific increases in muscle mass or lifting capacity, while for cutting, they could revolve around reducing body fat percentage or achieving a particular body composition.

Importantly, these goals must be adaptable. Bodybuilders need to regularly assess their progress and be willing to adjust their goals based on their body's response to training and diet. This flexibility is crucial, as rigid adherence to initial goals can lead to frustration or injury, particularly if those goals prove unrealistic.

Adjusting expectations and timelines is also essential. For instance, beginners might experience rapid gains in the initial stages of bulking (often referred to as "newbie gains"), but progress typically slows as they become more advanced. Similarly, during cutting, initial rapid weight loss may plateau, requiring adjustments in diet and training to continue making progress.

Setting short-term, process-oriented goals can also be beneficial. Rather than focusing solely on the end result (e.g., gaining 10 pounds of muscle), setting goals around consistent training habits or dietary adherence can provide a sense of accomplishment and help maintain motivation.

Mental Techniques for Sustained Motivation

Maintaining motivation during the demanding periods of intense bulking and strict cutting in bodybuilding requires effective mental techniques. Sports psychologists emphasize the importance of mental strategies in sustaining motivation under such challenging conditions.

One key technique is goal setting, where athletes set specific, measurable, achievable, relevant, and time-bound (SMART) goals. This approach provides clear targets and a sense of direction, which is crucial for maintaining focus and motivation. Research in the Journal of Applied Sport Psychology has shown that goal setting enhances athletes' motivation and performance (Locke & Latham, 2002).

Another technique is positive self-talk, which involves replacing negative thoughts with positive affirmations. This practice can boost an athlete's confidence and resilience, particularly during challenging phases like cutting, where physical and mental endurance are tested. The Journal of Sports Sciences reported that positive self-talk improves self-confidence and reduces performance anxiety in athletes.

Visualization, or mental rehearsal, is also a valuable technique for sustaining motivation. Athletes visualize themselves achieving their goals and overcoming obstacles, which enhances mental preparedness and maintains a positive outlook. A study in the Journal of Applied Sport Psychology demonstrated that visualization improves concentration and performance in competitive sports.

Mindfulness and meditation can further aid in maintaining motivation. These practices help athletes stay present and focused, reducing stress and preventing burnout. The International Journal of Sports Science & Coaching found that mindfulness meditation improves athletes' focus and reduces performance anxiety.

Part 4: Nutrition

Fueling Your Bodybuilding Journey

In the world of bodybuilding, nutrition is your ultimate weapon, your silent partner in the quest for muscle and strength. As you sweat it out in the gym, pushing your limits with every rep, your muscles are screaming for nourishment, and it's your job to feed them. This chapter, "The Fundamentals of Bodybuilding," lays down the foundation of what it means to be a bodybuilder, and how nutrition is the very essence of your journey.

Bodybuilding isn't a mere hobby; it's a lifestyle, a relentless pursuit of physical excellence. To understand its core, we must first delve into its history. Bodybuilding, as we know it today, wasn't born yesterday. It has a rich and gritty history that traces its roots back to ancient Greece, where Herculean physiques were celebrated. But it was in the late 19th century when the sport began to take its modern form. It became a spectacle, women flexing their sculpted bodies, showcasing strength, symmetry, and aesthetics. It wasn't just about being strong; it was about looking strong.

Fast forward to the present day, and bodybuilding has evolved into a multifaceted discipline. It's not just about bulging muscles and flashy poses; it's about sculpting your physique, pushing the limits of your body, and achieving the perfect blend of muscle and symmetry. It's a journey of dedication, discipline, and above all, nutrition.

You see, bodybuilding isn't a sprint; it's a marathon. And in this marathon, nutrition is your fuel. It's what powers your muscles to grow and recover. Without proper nutrition, your bodybuilding dreams are nothing but a house of cards waiting to collapse. You can lift all the weights in the world, but if you don't feed your body right, you'll never reach your true potential.

Now, let's get to the heart of the matter – the importance of nutrition in bodybuilding. It's not just about eating; it's about eating with a purpose. You're not shoving food down your throat; you're strategically fueling your body to achieve specific goals. Nutrition in bodybuilding isn't a one-size-fits-all concept. It's tailored to your unique needs, your body type, and your goals.

At the core of bodybuilding nutrition are macronutrients – protein, carbohydrates, and fats. These are the building blocks of your diet, and they play distinct roles in your bodybuilding journey.

Protein, the undisputed champion of macronutrients, is your muscle's best friend. It's the raw material your body needs to repair and grow muscle tissue. Every rep you do in the gym creates tiny tears in your muscle fibers. It's in the post-workout recovery phase that your muscles rebuild themselves, stronger and more massive than before. But they need protein to do so.

Sources of high-quality protein are your go-to weapons. Lean meats like chicken, turkey, and fish, along with dairy products like Greek yogurt and cottage cheese, should be your daily allies. Vegetarians can rely on sources like tofu, lentils, and quinoa to get their protein fix. But remember, it's not just about the quantity of protein; it's about the quality. Protein is your ammunition, so don't settle for anything less than the best.

Carbohydrates, often misunderstood and vilified, are the energy source that keeps your body firing on all cylinders. You've probably heard about low-carb diets and keto crazes, but in the world of bodybuilding, carbs are your friends. They provide the energy you need to fuel your workouts and recover afterward. Carbs are like the gasoline that powers a high-performance engine.

But not all carbs are created equal. Simple carbs, like those found in sugary snacks and sodas, will leave you crashing and burning. Complex carbs, on the other hand, are your secret weapon. Foods like brown rice, oats, sweet potatoes, and whole-grain bread provide a slow and steady release of energy, keeping you pumped throughout your grueling workouts.

Fats, often demonized in the dieting world, are essential for bodybuilders. They are the building blocks of hormones, including testosterone, which plays a critical role in muscle growth. But not all fats are created equal. Healthy fats, found in avocados, nuts, seeds, and fatty fish like salmon, are your allies in the quest for muscle. They also aid in the absorption of fat-soluble vitamins, ensuring your body gets the full nutritional benefit.

It's not about avoiding fats; it's about choosing the right ones. So, when someone tells you to go low-fat, you know better. Embrace the fats that fuel your body and enhance your muscle-building potential.

Now that you understand the role of macronutrients, it's time to put them into action. You're not just eating food; you're crafting a well-thought-out meal plan. The goal is to create a diet that provides the right balance of these macronutrients to support your bodybuilding objectives.

Balancing your macronutrients requires calculating your daily caloric needs. This isn't rocket science, but it does require some effort. You can't just eyeball your food and hope for the best. You need to know how many calories your body needs to maintain its current weight, and from there, you can adjust to achieve your goals.

There are various formulas and online calculators available to estimate your daily calorie needs. Once you have that number, you can determine how many of those calories should come from each macronutrient. For instance, a typical bodybuilding diet might consist of 40% carbohydrates, 30% protein, and 30% fats. This breakdown can be adjusted based on your specific goals.

Creating a meal plan based on these percentages can seem daunting, but it's crucial for success. It's like mapping out your battle strategy before entering the gym. With a well-structured plan, you'll have a clear path to your bodybuilding goals.

Timing is another crucial aspect of bodybuilding nutrition. You can't just eat haphazardly and expect results. Pre-workout nutrition sets the stage for your performance. You need a meal or snack that provides a good balance of carbohydrates and protein to fuel your workout and help you push through those heavy sets.

Post-workout nutrition is equally critical. After your intense training session, your muscles are starving for nutrients. This is the time to replenish your glycogen stores with carbohydrates and provide your muscles with the protein they need for recovery and growth. A post-workout shake or a well-balanced meal is your best bet.

Timing isn't just about the pre and post-workout periods; it's about consistency throughout the day. You should aim to eat every 3-4 hours to keep a steady flow of nutrients to your muscles. Skipping meals or going too long without eating can lead to muscle breakdown, the last thing you want as a bodybuilder.

Macronutrients for Muscle Growth

In the relentless world of bodybuilding, where iron meets sweat and determination collides with the weights, nutrition isn't just a part of the puzzle – it's the bedrock on which your success is built. This chapter, "Macronutrients for Muscle Growth," is all about the raw materials that fuel your body's transformation into a powerhouse of muscle and strength. In this no-nonsense guide, we'll dive straight into the core of bodybuilding nutrition, starting with the heavyweight champion of them all: protein.

Protein: The Cornerstone of Muscle Growth

Protein isn't just another nutrient; it's your ticket to muscle city. When you're pumping iron and pushing your body to the limits, you're essentially tearing down muscle fibers. It's in the recovery phase that your muscles rebuild and grow, and they need protein to do it.

Picture this: every rep, every set, and every drop of sweat are investments in your body's future. But without enough protein, those investments won't yield the returns you crave. Protein is the contractor that repairs the damaged muscle tissue, making it thicker, denser, and more powerful than before.

So, what's the deal with protein sources? Well, think of them as different tools in your muscle-building toolbox. Some are tried-and-true classics, while others are versatile newcomers.

- The Classics: Lean meats like chicken, turkey, and beef are your timeless protein allies. They're packed with essential amino acids, the building blocks of muscle. When you're looking to pack on mass, these should be your first choices. They're lean, mean, and muscle-building machines.

- Dairy Delights: Greek yogurt, cottage cheese, and milk are dairy powerhouses that are rich in protein. They also provide valuable calcium and other nutrients. If you're looking for a creamy way to fuel your muscles, these options are worth considering.

- Plant-Based Players: Not a fan of meat or dairy? No problem. Plant-based protein sources like tofu, lentils, chickpeas, and quinoa can be your go-to options. They offer protein with a side of fiber and an array of essential nutrients.

- Protein Powders: In the fast-paced world of bodybuilding, convenience matters. Protein powders, whether whey, casein, or plant-based, are quick and easy sources of protein. They're ideal for post-workout recovery when your muscles are hungry for nutrients.

But here's the deal-breaker – it's not just about the quantity of protein; it's also about the quality. Protein sources vary in terms of amino acid profiles and absorption rates. You want protein sources that are rich in essential amino acids and are easily digestible, ensuring your muscles get the most bang for their buck.

Now, let's talk numbers. How much protein do you need to feed those hungry muscles? The answer depends on various factors, including your body weight, age, activity level, and your specific bodybuilding goals.

For most bodybuilders, a good rule of thumb is to aim for around 1.2 to 2.2 grams of protein per kilogram of body weight daily. This range allows room for customization based on your unique needs. If you're looking to bulk up and pack on muscle, you may lean towards the higher end of the spectrum. If you're in a cutting phase and aiming to shed fat while preserving muscle, the lower end may suffice.

Carbohydrates: The Energy Source

Carbs often get a bad rap in the dieting world, but in the realm of bodybuilding, they're your secret weapon. Carbohydrates are your primary source of energy, the fuel that powers your workouts and recovery.

Picture your body as a high-performance car. It needs the right fuel to perform at its best. Complex carbohydrates are your premium octane. They provide a slow and steady release of energy, keeping you revved up throughout your grueling workouts.

But not all carbs are created equal. You've probably heard of simple carbs and complex carbs. Let's break it down.

- Simple Carbs: These are the sugary, quick-burning carbs found in candy, soda, and other processed junk. They might give you a temporary spike in energy, but they'll leave you crashing and burning soon after.

- Complex Carbs: These are your allies in the quest for muscle. Foods like brown rice, oats, sweet potatoes, whole-grain bread, and legumes provide a sustained release of energy. They keep you going strong, powering through set after set.

Now, here's the kicker – timing matters. Pre-workout nutrition is your opportunity to prime your body for a killer session at the gym. You want a meal or snack that provides a good balance of carbohydrates to fuel your workout and protein to kickstart muscle recovery. Think of it as loading up your car with premium fuel before a race.

Post-workout nutrition is equally crucial. After your intense training session, your muscles are starving for nutrients. This is the time to replenish your glycogen stores with carbohydrates and provide your muscles with the protein they need for recovery and growth. A post-workout shake or a well-balanced meal is your best bet.

But remember, carbohydrates aren't a license to gorge on pizza and pasta. The key is to choose complex carbs that are nutrient-dense and support your bodybuilding goals. You're not just fueling up; you're investing in your body's performance and progress.

- Fats: Essential for Hormone Production

- Fats have long been misunderstood and unfairly demonized in the world of nutrition. But in the world of bodybuilding, they're essential for hormone production, including testosterone, which plays a pivotal role in muscle growth.

- Think of fats as the oil that keeps the gears of your body's engine running smoothly. They're involved in various processes, including nutrient absorption, cell membrane health, and the production of vital hormones. Without enough healthy fats, your bodybuilding journey can hit a roadblock.

- But not all fats are created equal. There are the good guys – healthy fats – and the bad guys – trans fats and excessive saturated fats. Let's focus on the heroes of the story.

- Omega-3 Fatty Acids: Found in fatty fish like salmon, mackerel, and sardines, as well as walnuts and flaxseeds, omega-3 fatty acids are anti-inflammatory powerhouses. They support joint health, reduce muscle soreness, and aid in recovery.

- Monounsaturated Fats: Olive oil, avocados, and nuts are rich in monounsaturated fats. They promote heart health and provide a source of sustainable energy.

- Polyunsaturated Fats: These fats, found in sources like sunflower seeds, soybean oil, and fatty fish, are essential for overall health. They're also involved in maintaining the integrity of cell membranes.

Healthy fats not only keep your body's engine running but also aid in the absorption of fat-soluble vitamins like A, D, E, and K. So, when you're crafting your bodybuilding diet, don't skimp on fats; choose wisely.

Micronutrients and Supplements

In the unrelenting world of bodybuilding, where every lift, every repetition, and every drop of sweat counts, micronutrients and supplements are the secret arsenal that can elevate your journey to unprecedented heights. This chapter, "Micronutrients and Supplements," is not about the mainstream hype or miracle pills; it's about the nitty-gritty essentials that can make or break your pursuit of the ultimate physique.

Vitamins and Minerals for Muscle Health

Let's kick things off with the unsung heroes of nutrition – vitamins and minerals. Often overlooked in favor of macronutrients, these micronutrients are the foundation of your body's intricate machinery. They're the nuts and bolts that keep everything running smoothly.

- Vitamin A: Essential for maintaining healthy skin and mucous membranes, vitamin A also supports vision and immune function. It's found in foods like sweet potatoes, carrots, and spinach.

- Vitamin D: Known as the sunshine vitamin, vitamin D plays a crucial role in calcium absorption, bone health, and immune function. Get your fix from sunlight or fortified foods like fatty fish and fortified dairy products.

- Vitamin C: This antioxidant powerhouse supports collagen production, aids in wound healing, and boosts the immune system. Citrus fruits, strawberries, and bell peppers are excellent sources.

- Vitamin E: With its antioxidant properties, vitamin E helps protect cells from oxidative damage. Nuts, seeds, and vegetable oils are rich sources.

- Vitamin K: Vital for blood clotting and bone metabolism, vitamin K is found in leafy greens like kale, spinach, and broccoli.

- B Vitamins: This group includes B1 (thiamine), B2 (riboflavin), B3 (niacin), B5 (pantothenic acid), B6 (pyridoxine), B7 (biotin), B9 (folate), and B12 (cobalamin). They're involved in energy metabolism, red blood cell formation, and various cellular processes. Whole grains, meat, dairy, and leafy greens are good sources.

- Calcium: Essential for strong bones and muscle function, calcium can be found in dairy products, leafy greens, and fortified foods.

- Iron: Crucial for oxygen transport in the blood and muscle function, iron is abundant in red meat, poultry, fish, and legumes.

- Magnesium: This mineral is involved in muscle contraction and relaxation, energy production, and bone health. You can find it in nuts, seeds, whole grains, and leafy greens.

- Zinc: Essential for immune function and protein synthesis, zinc is prevalent in meat, dairy, nuts, and legumes.

- Selenium: An antioxidant that supports thyroid function and immune health, selenium is found in nuts, seeds, and seafood.

- Potassium: Crucial for muscle contractions and nerve impulses, potassium is abundant in bananas, potatoes, and citrus fruits.

These micronutrients aren't just fancy buzzwords. They're the vitamins and minerals your body needs to operate at peak performance. They're not optional; they're mandatory for the meticulous process of sculpting muscle and achieving your bodybuilding goals. Deficiencies can derail your progress faster than you can say "biceps."

The Role of Supplements

Now, let's talk about supplements – those pills, powders, and potions that promise to take your gains to the next level. Supplements can be a valuable addition to your bodybuilding toolkit, but they're not magic bullets. It's crucial to understand their role and use them wisely.

- Pre-Workout Supplements: These are designed to boost energy, focus, and endurance before hitting the gym. They often contain caffeine, creatine, and amino acids. While they can provide a temporary performance boost, they're not a substitute for a solid nutrition plan and should be used in moderation.

- Protein Supplements: Protein shakes and powders are convenient sources of protein, especially post-workout when your muscles need it the most. They're not a replacement for whole-food sources of protein but can be a useful tool for meeting your daily protein intake goals.

- Recovery Supplements: Branched-Chain Amino Acids (BCAAs) and glutamine are often marketed as recovery aids. While there's some evidence to suggest they may reduce muscle soreness and support recovery, they should complement a well-rounded diet rather than replace it.

- Vitamins and Minerals: If you have specific micronutrient deficiencies or struggle to meet your daily requirements through food alone, multivitamin and mineral supplements can be a safety net. However, it's best to get your nutrients from whole foods whenever possible.

- Fish Oil: Omega-3 fatty acids, found in fish oil supplements, have anti-inflammatory properties and can support joint and heart health. If you don't consume fatty fish regularly, consider this supplement.

- Creatine: Creatine is one of the most researched and proven supplements for increasing muscle mass and strength. It enhances ATP production, which can lead to improved performance during high-intensity, short-duration activities like weightlifting.

- Caffeine: Caffeine can increase alertness and energy levels, potentially improving workout performance. However, its effects can vary from person to person, and excessive caffeine intake can lead to negative side effects.

It's crucial to approach supplements with caution. While they can provide benefits, they should never replace a balanced diet rich in whole foods. Supplements are meant to supplement your nutrition, not substitute it. Before adding any supplement to your regimen, consult with a healthcare professional to ensure it's safe and suitable for your specific needs and goals.

Potential Risks and Benefits

In the quest for bodybuilding glory, it's tempting to view supplements as shortcuts to success. However, it's essential to weigh the potential risks against the benefits, especially when it comes to the unregulated supplement industry.

Benefits:

Convenience: Supplements can be a convenient way to meet your nutritional needs, especially when you're on the go or need a quick protein fix post-workout.

Performance Enhancement: Some supplements, like creatine, caffeine, and BCAAs, may enhance performance and recovery, allowing you to push harder in the gym.

Micronutrient Insurance: Multivitamin supplements can provide a safety net to cover potential micronutrient gaps in your diet.

Risks:

Quality Control: The supplement industry is notorious for poor quality control and mislabeling. Not all supplements contain what they claim, and some may even be contaminated with harmful substances.

Dependency: Relying too heavily on supplements can lead to a dependency mindset, neglecting the importance of whole foods in your diet.

Side Effects: Some supplements can cause adverse side effects or interact with medications. It's crucial to research and consult a healthcare professional before adding them to your regimen.

Financial Cost: Quality supplements can be expensive, and the cost can add up quickly if you're not careful.

In the end, the decision to use supplements should be a calculated one, based on your individual needs, goals, and the potential benefits they offer. Remember that no supplement can replace the foundation of proper nutrition, consistency in training, and restorative sleep.

Meal Planning and Timing

In the world of bodybuilding, where the pursuit of strength and aesthetics demands discipline and precision, the battle isn't just fought in the gym. It's waged on your plate, with every morsel of food, and every sip of liquid you consume. This chapter, "Meal Planning and Timing," is the blueprint for optimizing your nutrition strategy, ensuring that you fuel your body for peak performance and muscle growth without faltering in the face of dietary chaos.

The Importance of Meal Timing

In the battlefield of bodybuilding, timing is everything. It's not just about what you eat, but when you eat it. You wouldn't go to war without a strategy, and you shouldn't embark on your bodybuilding journey without a meal timing plan.

Pre-Workout Nutrition

Picture this: you're gearing up for a brutal training session, ready to unleash your inner beast on the weights. But there's an essential task at hand – fueling your body for the impending battle.

Pre-workout nutrition is your ticket to peak performance. It's about supplying your body with the right nutrients to ensure that you have the energy, focus, and strength needed to conquer your workout. The goal is simple: maximize your output in the gym, and you'll maximize your results.

Here's the breakdown:

Carbohydrates: Complex carbohydrates are your primary source of pre-workout fuel. They provide a steady release of energy to keep you going throughout your session. Think of them as the slow-burning fire that sustains your workout intensity.

Protein: While carbohydrates are the main event, protein plays a supporting role in pre-workout nutrition. It provides amino acids that help prevent muscle breakdown during your training session. It's like having body armor for your muscles.

Fats: Although fats aren't a primary focus of pre-workout nutrition, they can provide some sustained energy. However, keep fat intake moderate to avoid digestive discomfort during your workout.

Hydration: Hydration is non-negotiable. Dehydration can lead to decreased performance, fatigue, and even muscle cramps. Start your workout well-hydrated, and consider sipping on water or an electrolyte drink during your training.

The timing of your pre-workout meal or snack matters. You want to eat about 1 to 2 hours before hitting the gym, allowing your body to digest and absorb the nutrients effectively. If you're in a rush, a smaller snack 30 minutes before your workout can still provide a boost.

So, what does a pre-workout meal or snack look like in the real world?

Example Pre-Workout Meals:

- Grilled chicken breast with brown rice and steamed broccoli: A classic bodybuilder's choice, providing a balance of protein, complex carbs, and fiber for sustained energy.

- Greek yogurt with berries and a drizzle of honey: A quick and easy option rich in protein and carbohydrates.

- Oatmeal with sliced banana and a scoop of protein powder: A hearty meal with a blend of complex carbs and protein.

- Whole-grain toast with almond butter and a sprinkle of cinnamon: A simple yet effective choice that provides energy without being too heavy.

The key is to experiment and find what works best for you. Some people prefer a solid meal, while others opt for a light snack. Pay attention to how your body responds and adjust accordingly.

Intra-Workout Nutrition

During your intense training session, your muscles are working at full throttle, demanding fuel to sustain their performance. While you don't need a full-blown meal mid-workout, some strategic choices can keep your energy levels stable and support muscle recovery.

- Carbohydrate Sources: If your workout is exceptionally long or intense, consider sipping on a carbohydrate-based sports drink or consuming a carbohydrate gel to replenish glycogen stores and maintain energy levels.

- Amino Acids: Branched-Chain Amino Acids (BCAAs) or an essential amino acid supplement can help prevent muscle breakdown during extended workouts.

- Water: Stay hydrated throughout your workout. Dehydration can lead to decreased performance and muscle cramps.

- Intra-workout nutrition isn't always necessary for shorter training sessions, but it can be beneficial for marathon gym sessions or endurance training. Again, it's about customizing your strategy to match your specific needs.

- Post-Workout Nutrition: The Anabolic Window

You've just pushed your body to its limits, breaking down muscle fibers in the process. Now it's time for recovery, and post-workout nutrition is your secret weapon in the battle against muscle soreness and fatigue.

The post-workout period is often referred to as the "anabolic window." It's a window of opportunity when your muscles are primed for nutrient uptake, and the right choices can kick start the repair and growth process.

Here's what you need to know:

Protein: Post-workout, your muscles are hungry for protein. This is the time to provide them with the amino acids they need to rebuild and grow. Whey protein, due to its rapid digestion and absorption, is a popular choice, but other protein sources like lean meats, fish, eggs, or plant-based options work just as well.

Carbohydrates: Carbohydrates play a crucial role in post-workout nutrition as well. They replenish glycogen stores that were depleted during your workout and provide an insulin spike that can enhance protein uptake. Fast-digesting carbohydrates like white rice, potatoes, or simple sugars can be effective choices.

Hydration: Rehydrate with water or an electrolyte drink to replace fluids lost during your workout.

Timing: The post-workout meal or shake should be consumed ideally within 30 minutes to 2 hours after your workout. This timing can maximize the benefits of the anabolic window.

Example Post-Workout Meals:

- Grilled salmon with quinoa and steamed asparagus: A well-rounded meal providing protein, complex carbs, and essential nutrients.

- Protein shake with whey protein, a banana, and a tablespoon of honey: A quick and convenient option that hits the mark for protein and carbohydrates.

- Turkey sandwich on whole-grain bread with plenty of veggies: A balanced choice that combines protein, carbohydrates, and fiber.

- Vegan protein bowl with brown rice, tofu, and mixed vegetables: A plant-based option rich in protein and complex carbs.

Remember that your post-workout meal doesn't need to be overly complicated. The goal is to provide your body with the nutrients it needs for recovery and growth. Tailor your choices to your dietary preferences and sensitivities.

Meal Frequency: The 3-4 Hour Rule

In the world of bodybuilding, consistency is king. It's not just about what you eat but how often you eat. The 3-4 hour rule is a fundamental principle of meal frequency for bodybuilders. Here's how it works:

- Eat Every 3-4 Hours: You should aim to eat a meal or snack every 3-4 hours throughout the day. This consistent meal frequency helps maintain a steady supply of nutrients to support muscle growth and recovery.

- Prevents Muscle Breakdown: Eating regularly prevents your body from going into a catabolic state, where it breaks down muscle tissue for energy. By providing a constant stream of nutrients, you keep your muscles in an anabolic, or growth-promoting, state.

- Optimizes Nutrient Timing: The 3-4 hour rule aligns with the timing of your workouts. By having a meal or snack within a few hours of training, you ensure that your body has the necessary fuel to perform at its best during exercise. Post-workout, another meal or snack replenishes glycogen stores and provides the amino acids needed for muscle repair and growth.

- Balances Blood Sugar: Consistent meal frequency helps stabilize blood sugar levels. Sharp spikes and crashes in blood sugar can lead to cravings, mood swings, and energy slumps. By eating every 3-4 hours, you maintain steady energy levels and reduce the risk of overindulging in unhealthy snacks.

- Supports Metabolism: Regular meals and snacks keep your metabolism revved up. Your body burns calories while digesting and processing food, and frequent eating helps maintain this calorie-burning process throughout the day.

- Prevents Overeating: When you allow too much time between meals, you're more likely to become ravenous and overeat during your next meal. By eating every 3-4 hours, you can better control portion sizes and make healthier food choices.

- Promotes Hydration: Meal frequency also encourages regular hydration. Many bodybuilders forget that water intake is as crucial as food. By eating frequently, you're reminded to stay hydrated, supporting digestion and overall health.

- Creates Routine and Structure: Consistency in meal frequency creates a structured daily routine. This structure can help you plan your workouts, meals, and other activities, making it easier to stay on track with your bodybuilding goals.

- Now, while the 3-4 hour rule is a solid guideline, it's essential to adapt it to your individual needs and schedule. Some people may thrive with more frequent meals, while others may find three main meals and a couple of snacks to be sufficient. The key is to listen to your body and ensure you're meeting your daily calorie and nutrient requirements.

- Incorporate lean proteins, complex carbohydrates, and healthy fats into your meals and snacks to support muscle growth, energy, and overall health. Remember that portion control is vital, even when eating frequently, to avoid excessive calorie intake.

- Consistency is the cornerstone of success in bodybuilding. Whether you're in the bulking or cutting phase, adhering to a regular meal frequency is a non-negotiable part of your nutrition strategy. Embrace the 3-4 hour rule as a fundamental principle in your bodybuilding journey, and watch how it contributes to your progress, one meal at a time.

Nutritional Strategies for Bulking and Cutting

The chapter at hand, "Nutritional Strategies for Bulking and Cutting," is the unwavering blueprint for sculpting your physique, whether you're adding mass or chiseling it to perfection. It's not about following the latest fad or blindly cramming calories; it's about calculated and ruthless nutrition tactics that will propel you towards your bodybuilding goals.

The Bulking Phase: Building the Foundation of Power

Bulking isn't about mindlessly gorging on everything in sight. It's a calculated and strategic approach to building muscle and strength. In this phase, you're in a caloric surplus, consuming more calories than your body burns. The goal is to provide your muscles with an abundance of nutrients to fuel growth, repair, and recovery.

- Caloric Surplus: To bulk effectively, you need a surplus of calories. But don't take it as a license to eat everything in sight.

The surplus should be controlled, ensuring that the additional calories go towards muscle growth, not fat storage.

- Macronutrient Ratios: While your macros (protein, carbohydrates, and fats) will largely remain the same, you may adjust the ratios slightly. Protein remains crucial for muscle repair, while carbohydrates provide the energy needed to fuel those intense workouts. Healthy fats should be a part of your diet, but their role is supportive, not primary.

- Protein: Aim to maintain a protein intake of around 1.2 to 2.2 grams per kilogram of body weight. Protein is your muscle's best friend, ensuring you recover and grow optimally during the bulking phase.

- Carbohydrates: Carbs should make up a significant portion of your diet, providing energy for your workouts and aiding in muscle recovery. Complex carbohydrates are your allies, delivering sustained energy without the sugar crashes.

- Fats: Healthy fats are essential for overall health, including hormone production, but keep them in moderation. They're supplementary, helping you meet your caloric needs.

- Meal Timing: The 3-4 hour meal frequency rule still applies. Consistent nutrient intake keeps your body in an anabolic state, conducive to muscle growth.

Examples of Bulking Meals:

- Grilled chicken breast with quinoa, roasted sweet potatoes, and a side of steamed broccoli: A balanced meal providing protein, complex carbs, and fiber.

- Whole-grain pasta with lean ground beef and a tomato-based sauce: A hearty meal rich in protein and complex carbs.

- Protein shake with whey protein, oats, banana, and almond butter: A nutrient-dense option for an additional calorie boost.

The Cutting Phase: Chiseling Your Masterpiece

Once you've built the foundation of muscle mass during the bulking phase, it's time to reveal the masterpiece beneath. The cutting phase is all about shedding body fat while preserving your hard-earned muscle. It's a meticulous dance between calorie restriction and macronutrient optimization.

Caloric Deficit: Cutting involves consuming fewer calories than your body burns, creating a caloric deficit. However, it's crucial to strike a balance – too much of a deficit can lead to muscle loss.

Protein: Your protein intake remains high during cutting to preserve muscle mass. Aim for the same protein range as in the bulking phase.

Carbohydrates: Carbs should still be a part of your diet but may be adjusted downward. Focus on complex carbs to keep you feeling full and energized.

Fats: Healthy fats remain in your diet, as they support overall health and hormone balance. They can also aid in satiety during calorie restriction.

Meal Timing: The 3-4 hour rule continues to be your guide during the cutting phase. Consistency in meal frequency is vital to maintain muscle and curb cravings.

Examples of Cutting Meals:

- Grilled salmon with a side of quinoa and steamed asparagus: A lean protein source combined with complex carbs and fiber for satiety.

- Salad with grilled chicken, mixed greens, and a vinaigrette dressing: A low-calorie, high-protein meal that keeps you feeling full.

- Stir-fried tofu with broccoli and brown rice: A plant-based option rich in protein and complex carbs.

Cardio and Training: Cardio can be a valuable tool during the cutting phase to enhance calorie burning. High-intensity interval training (HIIT) is particularly effective for fat loss. However, don't overdo it, as excessive cardio can lead to muscle loss.

Supplements: During cutting, supplements like BCAAs and whey protein can help preserve muscle and manage cravings. Remember, though, supplements are a complement to your diet, not a replacement.

Hydration: Staying hydrated is crucial during cutting, as thirst can sometimes be mistaken for hunger. Drink plenty of water throughout the day.

Tracking Progress: Keep a close eye on your progress during the cutting phase. Regular assessments of body composition, such as body fat percentage and muscle mass, can help you fine-tune your approach.

Cheat Meals: While discipline is essential, occasional cheat meals can be a mental relief and help prevent binging. Keep them controlled and don't let them derail your progress.

Cycling: Some bodybuilders employ calorie cycling during the cutting phase, alternating between higher and lower-calorie days. This approach can help prevent metabolic adaptation and maintain muscle.

Refeeding: Periodic refeeding days, where you temporarily increase your calorie intake, can help reset hormone levels and alleviate some of the metabolic slowdown associated with prolonged calorie restriction.

The key to success in the cutting phase is discipline and consistency. It's not an easy journey, and it demands mental fortitude, but the results are worth the sacrifice. Cutting is about revealing the masterpiece you've sculpted during bulking, and the sharper your tools, the more impeccable your creation will be.

Specialized Diets for Bodybuilders

Nutrition is the unsung hero that separates the champions from the rest. This chapter, "Specialized Diets for Bodybuilders," isn't about quick fixes or trendy diets; it's about ruthless and calculated approaches to nutrition that can take your physique to the next level. If you're ready to push your limits and sculpt your body into a work of art, read on.

Ketogenic Diet: Carving out the Fat

The ketogenic diet, often dubbed "keto," has gained notoriety for its remarkable ability to shed body fat like a hot knife through butter. This high-fat, low-carb diet is a weapon of choice for bodybuilders looking to get leaner while preserving muscle mass.

In a ketogenic diet:

- Carbohydrates are severely restricted: Typically, carbs make up only about 5-10% of total daily calories. This restriction forces your body to rely on fat for fuel instead of glucose from carbs.

- Fats take the spotlight: Approximately 70-80% of your daily calories come from healthy fats like avocados, nuts, seeds, and oils. These fats become the primary energy source.

- Protein remains moderate: Protein intake hovers around 15-20% of daily calories. It's sufficient to support muscle maintenance and growth.

The ketogenic diet induces a state called ketosis, where your body starts producing ketones from fat breakdown. Ketones serve as an alternative fuel source for your muscles and brain. During this process, your body becomes incredibly efficient at burning stored fat for energy, making it an excellent choice for cutting phases.

However, the keto diet isn't a walk in the park. It demands strict adherence, and the initial transition can be mentally and physically challenging as your body adapts to the absence of carbs. It's not a long-term solution, but when used strategically during cutting phases, it can yield remarkable results in shedding body fat while preserving muscle.

Cyclical Ketogenic Diet: The Best of Both Worlds

For those who crave carbohydrates, the cyclical ketogenic diet (CKD) offers a compromise. CKD involves cycling between periods of strict keto and short "carb-loading" phases.

Here's how it works:

- Keto Phase: During this phase, which can last anywhere from 5 to 6 days, you follow a strict ketogenic diet, similar to what was described earlier. Your carb intake is minimal.

- Carb-Loading Phase: This is the break you've been waiting for. On this day (or sometimes two days), you load up on carbs, sometimes exceeding your daily calorie needs. This carb influx refills muscle glycogen stores and provides a mental and physical boost.

CKD offers the metabolic benefits of ketosis while providing periodic relief from carb restriction. It's a strategy favored by some bodybuilders to enjoy the best of both worlds – the fat-shredding power of keto and the muscle-sparing properties of carb refeeds.

Intermittent Fasting: Fasting for Gains

Intermittent fasting (IF) is a nutritional strategy that's gained popularity in recent years, thanks to its simplicity and potential health benefits. For bodybuilders, it can be a valuable tool for managing calorie intake, improving insulin sensitivity, and supporting fat loss.

IF involves cycling between periods of fasting and eating. Here are some common IF approaches:

- 16/8 Method: This method involves fasting for 16 hours each day and limiting your eating window to 8 hours. Most people achieve this by skipping breakfast and eating their first meal around noon.

- 5:2 Method: In this approach, you eat normally for five days of the week and limit calorie intake to around 500-600 calories on the remaining two days.

- Eat-Stop-Eat: With this method, you fast for a full 24 hours once or twice a week. For example, you might eat dinner at 7 pm one day and not eat again until 7 pm the following day.

- Alternate-Day Fasting: This approach involves alternating between days of regular eating and days of fasting or consuming very few calories.

Intermittent fasting isn't about restricting specific food groups or macronutrients; it's about controlling when you eat. During the fasting period, your body taps into stored fat for energy, potentially aiding in fat loss. It can also improve insulin sensitivity, which is beneficial for overall health and muscle growth.

However, IF may not be suitable for everyone, especially those with specific dietary requirements or training schedules. It's essential to tailor the fasting approach to your individual needs and goals.

Vegetarian and Vegan Diets: Plant-Powered Gains

Contrary to the misconception that bodybuilding relies solely on animal protein, vegetarian and vegan diets can also be powerful tools for muscle growth and strength. With careful planning and strategic food choices, plant-powered bodybuilders can achieve remarkable results.

Here's how it's done:

- Protein Sources: Plant-based protein sources become the cornerstone of your diet. These include tofu, tempeh, seitan, legumes (such as lentils, chickpeas, and black beans), and plant-based protein powders. Nuts and seeds are also excellent protein sources.

- Amino Acid Balance: To ensure you're getting all the essential amino acids, it's crucial to diversify your protein sources. Combining different plant proteins, like beans and rice, can help achieve a balanced amino acid profile.

- Iron-Rich Foods: Plant-based diets can provide plenty of iron through foods like dark leafy greens, fortified cereals, and legumes. Iron is essential for oxygen transport, which is crucial during workouts.

- B12 Supplementation: Vitamin B12 is primarily found in animal products, so many vegetarians and vegans need to supplement or consume B12-fortified foods to avoid deficiencies.

- Caloric Surplus: To build muscle, you'll still need a caloric surplus, just like any other bodybuilder. This means consuming more calories than you burn to support muscle growth.

Vegetarian and vegan bodybuilders can enjoy the same benefits as their omnivorous counterparts – increased muscle mass, strength, and improved overall health. With proper planning and a keen eye on nutrient intake, plant-powered bodybuilders can thrive in the gym and on the stage.

Carb Cycling: Timing Your Carbs for Gains

Carb cycling is a strategic approach to nutrition that involves alternating between high-carb and low-carb days. It's a favorite among bodybuilders for optimizing energy levels, supporting muscle growth, and managing body fat.

The premise of carb cycling is straightforward:

- High-Carb Days: On these days, you increase your carbohydrate intake to support intense workouts and refuel muscle glycogen stores. High-carb days are often aligned with your most grueling

Staying Hydrated and Monitoring Progress

In bodybuilding, two crucial elements often take a back seat: hydration and progress monitoring. Neglecting these can be the Achilles' heel that undermines your journey to sculpting the ultimate physique. In this chapter, we'll delve into the unsung heroes of bodybuilding – staying hydrated and monitoring progress. No fluff, no frills, just raw knowledge to elevate your game.

Hydration: The Overlooked Game Changer

Water is the unsung hero of your bodybuilding arsenal. While you're busy counting reps and tracking macros, hydration often slips through the cracks. Yet, it's one of the most critical components of your success. Without proper hydration, your body can't perform at its peak, and your gains will suffer.

The Importance of Hydration

Picture this: you're in the midst of an intense workout, beads of sweat pouring down your face, and your muscles pushing to their limit. Every movement is a testament to your dedication. But there's an often-underestimated factor at play – your hydration status.

Hydration is not just about quenching your thirst; it's about ensuring that your body functions optimally. Here's why it matters:

- Muscle Function: Dehydration can lead to muscle cramps and decreased muscle contractions, hampering your performance.

- Temperature Regulation: Sweating is your body's cooling mechanism. Without sufficient water, you risk overheating, which can be dangerous during intense workouts.

- Energy Levels: Even mild dehydration can lead to fatigue and reduced energy levels, making it harder to push through your training sessions.

- Recovery: Proper hydration is essential for post-workout recovery. It helps transport nutrients to your muscles, aiding in repair and growth.

- Cognitive Function: Dehydration can impair focus and cognitive function, affecting your workout intensity and form.

How Much Water Do You Need?

The age-old advice of drinking eight 8-ounce glasses of water a day is a good starting point for the average person. However, bodybuilders often have greater hydration needs due to their intense training regimens and increased sweat rates.

A more personalized approach is to calculate your water needs based on your body weight. As a general guideline, aim for about 30-35 milliliters of water per kilogram of body weight per day. For example, if you weigh 70 kilograms (154 pounds), you'd need approximately 2,100 to 2,450 milliliters of water daily.

Keep in mind that individual factors like climate, activity level, and sweat rate can affect your hydration requirements. On intense workout days, you may need to drink even more to compensate for fluid loss.

Signs of Dehydration

Detecting dehydration early is crucial to prevent its detrimental effects. Here are some common signs to watch out for:

- Thirst: The most apparent signal that your body needs water.

- Dark Urine: Dark yellow or amber-colored urine is a sign of dehydration. Your urine should be pale yellow.

- Dry Mouth and Skin: Dry or sticky feeling in your mouth and skin can indicate dehydration.

- Fatigue: If you feel unusually tired during your workout or throughout the day, it could be due to dehydration.

- Headache: Dehydration can trigger headaches and migraines.

- Muscle Cramps: Frequent muscle cramps, especially during exercise, may be a sign of inadequate hydration.

Strategies for Staying Hydrated

Now that you understand the importance of hydration let's dive into some strategies to ensure you stay adequately hydrated:

- Drink Throughout the Day: Don't wait until you're thirsty to start drinking. Sip water consistently throughout the day.

- Pre-Workout Hydration: Drink a glass of water about 2 hours before your workout to ensure you start your training session well-hydrated.

- During Workout: Sip on water or an electrolyte drink during your workout, especially if it's intense or lengthy. Electrolyte drinks can help replace lost minerals through sweat.

- Post-Workout Rehydration: After your workout, rehydrate with water or a recovery drink to replace fluid losses.

- Monitor Urine Color: Keep an eye on the color of your urine. If it's pale yellow, you're likely well-hydrated. Dark yellow or amber urine is a sign to drink more water.

- Consider Your Environment: Hot and humid conditions can increase sweat rates, so you'll need to drink more to compensate.

- Electrolytes: If you're sweating excessively, especially in a hot climate, consider incorporating electrolyte drinks or foods high in electrolytes, like bananas or coconut water, into your regimen.

Hydration is the foundation of your bodybuilding journey. It's not an option; it's a necessity. Neglecting it can undermine your hard work and dedication in the gym. So, remember to drink up, even when the iron is calling your name.

Monitoring Progress: Your North Star

In the ruthless world of bodybuilding, progress isn't just a goal; it's the guiding light that keeps you on track. Yet, many aspiring bodybuilders stumble in the dark, not knowing how to navigate their journey. That's where progress monitoring comes in – your North Star in the constellation of gains.

Why Monitor Progress

Imagine setting sail on a treacherous sea without a compass or map. You'd be lost in the vastness, drifting aimlessly. The same holds for bodybuilding. Monitoring your progress is your compass, guiding you through the turbulent waters of training and nutrition.

Here's why it matters:

- Motivation: Tracking your progress can be incredibly motivating. It allows you to see the fruits of your labor and provides a sense of achievement.

- Adjustments: Without monitoring, you're flying blind. Progress tracking helps you identify what's working and what isn't, allowing you to make necessary adjustments to your training and nutrition.

- Plateau Prevention: It's not uncommon to hit plateaus in your bodybuilding journey. Progress monitoring helps you recognize when progress stalls so you can pivot and keep moving forward.

- Accountability: When you're tracking your progress, you're less likely to skip workouts or deviate from your nutrition plan. It creates a sense of accountability to your goals.

What to Monitor

Progress monitoring goes beyond simply stepping on a scale. While body weight is one factor, it's far from the only one. Here's what you should be tracking:

- Body Weight: Your weight can provide insights into changes in muscle mass and body fat. However, it's not the sole indicator of progress, as fluctuations can occur due to various factors.

- Body Measurements: Tracking measurements of key areas like chest, waist, hips, arms, and legs can give you a more comprehensive view of your body's transformation. These measurements can help you identify changes in specific muscle groups and areas where you might be losing fat.

- Body Fat Percentage: Measuring your body fat percentage is crucial for understanding how your body composition is evolving. It's a more accurate reflection of progress than body weight alone, as it accounts for changes in muscle and fat.

- Strength and Performance: Keep a close eye on your strength and performance in the gym. Are you lifting heavier weights, completing more reps, or improving your workout intensity? These improvements signal muscle growth and increased fitness levels.

- Energy Levels: Your energy levels are a valuable indicator of your overall health. As your nutrition and training plan progress, you should experience increased energy and endurance during workouts and throughout the day.

- Recovery and Soreness: Pay attention to how quickly you recover from workouts and the level of soreness you experience. Improved recovery and reduced soreness can indicate that your nutrition plan is supporting muscle repair and growth.

- Mood and Mental Clarity: Nutrition doesn't just affect your body; it has a significant impact on your mind. Monitor changes in mood, mental clarity, and focus. A well-balanced diet can enhance your cognitive function and overall well-being.

- Sleep Quality: Adequate sleep is essential for recovery and muscle growth. Track your sleep quality and duration. Improved sleep patterns are a positive sign that your nutrition and training are on the right track.

- Skin Health: The condition of your skin can also reflect your nutritional status. Healthy, clear skin can be a sign of a well-balanced diet with adequate hydration.

- Hunger and Appetite: Pay attention to your hunger and appetite cues. A well-structured nutrition plan should help regulate your appetite and reduce cravings for unhealthy foods.

- Digestive Health: Digestive issues can hinder nutrient absorption. Monitor your digestive health and make adjustments to your diet if you experience discomfort, bloating, or irregularity.

- While these indicators are essential for tracking progress, remember that changes won't happen overnight. Patience and consistency are your allies on this journey. Use these markers to make informed adjustments to your nutrition plan and training regimen as you work toward your bodybuilding goals. The path to mastery is marked by these small steps and incremental improvements, and every bit of progress is a step closer to the body you're sculpting.

Common Mistakes and Pitfalls

In the relentless pursuit of the perfect physique, where sweat and iron are your constant companions, there's little room for error. Yet, even the most dedicated bodybuilders can stumble and fall prey to common mistakes and pitfalls along the way. In this chapter, we'll expose these pitfalls, not to dwell on them, but to arm you with the knowledge to sidestep these traps and keep forging ahead.

Neglecting Proper Warm-Ups and Cool-Downs

Picture this: you walk into the gym, fueled with determination, ready to conquer the weights. You head straight to the squat rack, load up the bar, and dive into your working sets. Sounds familiar? It's a common scenario, but it's also a recipe for disaster.

The Mistake: Neglecting proper warm-ups and cool-downs.

Why It's a Pitfall: Failing to warm up adequately can increase the risk of injuries and reduce your performance during your workout. Conversely, skipping a cool-down can lead to delayed onset muscle soreness (DOMS) and hinder recovery.

The Solution: Prioritize your warm-up and cool-down routines. Start with 5-10 minutes of light aerobic activity to increase blood flow to your muscles. Follow it with dynamic stretching or mobility exercises to prepare your body for the workout ahead. After your workout, dedicate another 5-10 minutes to static stretching and foam rolling to aid recovery.

Overtraining and Under-Recovery

In the pursuit of gains, more is not always better. Many bodybuilders fall victim to the belief that relentless training and minimal rest will accelerate progress. However, this approach can lead to a vicious cycle of overtraining and under-recovery.

The Mistake: Overtraining and neglecting the importance of recovery.

Why It's a Pitfall: Overtraining can lead to fatigue, decreased performance, increased risk of injuries, and even hormonal imbalances. It hampers your body's ability to repair and grow muscle.

The Solution: Prioritize rest and recovery as much as your training sessions. Ensure you're getting adequate sleep, as it's during slumber that your body performs its most significant recovery and repair work. Implement planned deload weeks in your training program to allow your body to recuperate fully. Listen to your body; if you're feeling excessively fatigued or experiencing chronic soreness, it's a sign to ease up and prioritize recovery.

Ignoring Proper Form

In the world of bodybuilding, lifting heavy is a badge of honor. However, this pursuit of weightlifting supremacy can often come at the expense of proper form and technique.

The Mistake: Ignoring proper form and prioritizing lifting heavier weights.

Why It's a Pitfall: Neglecting form can lead to injuries and limit muscle activation. It shifts the focus from targeted muscle groups to secondary muscles, reducing the effectiveness of your exercises.

The Solution: Prioritize proper form above all else. Focus on controlled, full-range-of-motion repetitions. Reduce the weight if needed to maintain good form. If you're unsure about your technique, seek guidance from a qualified trainer or use mirrors to visually assess your form during exercises.

Neglecting Nutrient Timing

Nutrition is the lifeblood of bodybuilding, and timing plays a crucial role in optimizing your results. Yet, many bodybuilders overlook the significance of nutrient timing, missing out on the full potential of their nutrition strategy.

The Mistake: Neglecting nutrient timing, such as pre-workout and post-workout nutrition.

Why It's a Pitfall: Timing your nutrients strategically can enhance workout performance, muscle recovery, and growth. Neglecting this aspect can leave gains on the table.

The Solution: Prioritize pre-workout and post-workout nutrition. Consume a balanced meal or snack 1-2 hours before your workout, focusing on a combination of carbohydrates and protein. After your workout, have a post-workout meal or shake within 30 minutes to 2 hours, emphasizing protein and fast-digesting carbohydrates to kickstart recovery.

Excessive Supplementation

The supplement industry is a billion-dollar business, and it's easy to fall into the trap of believing that a cabinet full of pills and powders will be the key to your success.

The Mistake: Relying too heavily on supplements.

Why It's a Pitfall: Supplements are meant to complement your diet, not replace it. Depending on supplements can lead to nutrient imbalances and financial strain.

The Solution: Prioritize whole foods as the foundation of your nutrition. Supplements should be used strategically to fill gaps in your diet, not as a primary source of nutrients. Focus on essentials like protein powder, creatine, and branched-chain amino acids (BCAAs), but don't neglect a well-balanced diet.

Inconsistent Tracking

In the world of bodybuilding, consistency is king. Whether it's tracking your workouts, nutrition, or progress, inconsistency can lead to stagnation.

The Mistake: Inconsistent tracking of workouts, nutrition, and progress.

Why It's a Pitfall: Inconsistency makes it challenging to identify what's working and what isn't. It hinders your ability to make informed adjustments to your training and nutrition plan.

The Solution: Prioritize consistency in tracking. Keep a detailed workout journal, recording exercises, sets, reps, and weights. Track your daily nutrition intake, including macros and calories. Take regular progress photos and measurements to monitor changes in your physique. This data will be invaluable in fine-tuning your approach and ensuring steady progress.

Neglecting Mobility and Flexibility

In the quest for muscle and strength, flexibility and mobility are often disregarded. However, these aspects are crucial for injury prevention and optimal performance.

The Mistake: Neglecting mobility and flexibility training.

Why It's a Pitfall: Poor mobility and flexibility can lead to imbalances, reduced range of motion, and an increased risk of injuries. It can also hinder your ability to perform exercises with proper form.

The Solution: Prioritize mobility and flexibility exercises in your routine. Include dynamic stretches and mobility drills in your warm-up to prepare your muscles and joints for exercise. Dedicate time to static stretching and foam rolling in your cool-down to enhance flexibility and aid recovery.

Progress isn't always a linear path. You'll encounter setbacks, challenges, and moments of self-doubt. However, by learning from the common mistakes and pitfalls that many bodybuilders face, you can navigate your journey with greater confidence and success. Remember, it's not about avoiding these pitfalls entirely; it's about recognizing them, learning from them, and using them as stepping stones toward your ultimate goal: mastery of your body and your craft.

Example Meal Plans

In this chapter, we won't delve into the intricacies of theory or dabble in the hypothetical; we'll cut through the noise and lay bare the practicality of nutrition mastery with concrete example meal plans. No frills, no fluff, just the battle-tested fuel that will propel you closer to your bodybuilding goals.

Meal Plan 1: Fuel for Bulking

Bulking isn't an invitation for reckless eating; it's a calculated assault on muscle growth. Here's a meal plan that provides the sustenance needed to add mass without sacrificing quality.

Meal 1: Breakfast

- Scrambled Eggs: 3 large eggs cooked in olive oil for healthy fats and protein.

- Whole-Grain Toast: 2 slices for complex carbs and fiber.

- Spinach and Tomato: A side of veggies for vitamins and minerals.

Meal 2: Mid-Morning Snack

- Greek Yogurt: 1 cup for protein and probiotics.

- Mixed Berries: A handful for antioxidants and flavor.

Meal 3: Lunch

- Grilled Chicken Breast: 6 ounces for lean protein.

- Quinoa: 1 cup for complex carbs and fiber.

- Steamed Broccoli: A side of greens for nutrients.

Meal 4: Pre-Workout

- Protein Shake: 1 scoop of whey protein for fast-digesting amino acids.

- Banana: A quick source of energy.

Meal 5: Post-Workout

- Salmon: 6 ounces for protein and healthy fats.

- Brown Rice: 1 cup for sustained energy.

- Asparagus: A side of greens for vitamins and fiber.

Meal 6: Dinner

- Lean Beef Steak: 6 ounces for protein and iron.

- Sweet Potatoes: 1 cup for complex carbs and beta-carotene.

- Mixed Vegetables: A side of colorful veggies for vitamins.

Meal 7: Evening Snack

- Cottage Cheese: 1 cup for casein protein (slow-digesting).

- Almonds: A small handful for healthy fats.

Meal Plan 2: Precision for Cutting

Cutting is about sculpting your masterpiece by shedding excess body fat while preserving muscle. This meal plan provides the precision needed to reveal the chiseled physique beneath.

Meal 1: Breakfast

- Oatmeal: 1 cup for complex carbs and fiber.

- Egg Whites: 4 egg whites for protein.

- Spinach: A handful for added nutrients.

Meal 2: Mid-Morning Snack

- Protein Shake: 1 scoop of whey protein.

- Almonds: A small handful for healthy fats.

Meal 3: Lunch

- Grilled Turkey Breast: 6 ounces for lean protein.

- Quinoa Salad: 1 cup for complex carbs and fiber.

- Mixed Greens: A generous portion for vitamins.

Meal 4: Pre-Workout

- Greek Yogurt: 1 cup for protein.

- Berries: A handful for antioxidants.

Meal 5: Post-Workout

- Chicken Breast: 6 ounces for lean protein.

- Brown Rice: 1 cup for complex carbs.

- Broccoli: A side of greens for vitamins and fiber.

Meal 6: Dinner

- Salmon: 6 ounces for protein and healthy fats.

- Asparagus: A side of greens for nutrients.

- Quinoa: 1/2 cup for additional carbs.

Meal 7: Evening Snack

- Cottage Cheese: 1 cup for casein protein.

- Walnuts: A small handful for healthy fats.

Meal Plan 3: Vegetarian Power

Contrary to the misconception that bodybuilding relies solely on animal protein, a vegetarian meal plan can provide the power needed for muscle growth and strength.

Meal 1: Breakfast

- Scrambled Tofu: Tofu cooked with veggies for protein and nutrients.

- Whole-Grain Toast: 2 slices for complex carbs.

- Spinach and Tomato: A side of greens for vitamins.

Meal 2: Mid-Morning Snack

- Greek Yogurt: 1 cup for protein.

- Mixed Berries: A handful for antioxidants.

Meal 3: Lunch

- Tempeh Stir-Fry: Tempeh with mixed vegetables for protein and fiber.

- Brown Rice: 1 cup for complex carbs.

Meal 4: Pre-Workout

- Protein Shake: 1 scoop of plant-based protein.

- Banana: A quick source of energy.

Meal 5: Post-Workout

- Chickpea Salad: Chickpeas with veggies for protein and fiber.

- Quinoa: 1/2 cup for additional carbs.

Meal 6: Dinner

- Lentil Curry: Lentils cooked with spices and served with brown rice for protein and complex carbs.

- Mixed Vegetables: A side of greens for vitamins.

Meal 7: Evening Snack

- Cottage Cheese: 1 cup for casein protein.

- Almonds: A small handful for healthy fats.

These meal plans are not set in stone but serve as templates to demonstrate the practicality of a balanced nutrition strategy. The key to success is consistency and adaptability. Tailor your meals to your preferences and dietary requirements while adhering to your macro and calorie targets. Remember, nutrition mastery is about the relentless pursuit of your bodybuilding goals, one meal at a time.

Conclusion

The knowledge you've acquired throughout these pages is not a one-size-fits-all solution, nor is it a guarantee of instant success. It's a toolbox filled with the tools and strategies you need to master your nutrition and elevate your bodybuilding game. It's a collection of insights gained from years of sweat, sacrifice, and relentless pursuit of excellence.

But here's the unvarnished truth: the most powerful tool in that toolbox is you – your discipline, your consistency, and your unyielding determination. Without these, no amount of knowledge or advice can propel you forward. The road to bodybuilding mastery is paved with unwavering dedication and the refusal to settle for mediocrity.

So, as you step out of these pages and back into the world of weight plates and protein shakes, carry with you the understanding that success in bodybuilding isn't about perfection; it's about progress. It's not about avoiding mistakes but learning from them. It's not about shortcuts or quick fixes but the relentless pursuit of your best self.

In every meal you prepare, every rep you lift, and every step you take on this journey, remember that you are the sculptor, and your body is the canvas. With each choice you make, you chisel away the excess, revealing the masterpiece within.

As we reach the conclusion of this exploration into the world of women's bodybuilding, it is clear that this sport is much more than a mere showcase of physical strength and muscular development. It is a testament to resilience, a journey of empowerment, and a narrative of breaking barriers. Women's bodybuilding transcends the lifting of weights and the sculpting of physiques; it challenges deep-seated stereotypes, redefines femininity, and celebrates the extraordinary capabilities of women.

Throughout the chapters, we have seen the diverse paths that lead women to the world of bodybuilding. From overcoming personal adversities and health challenges to shattering societal norms and achieving professional excellence, each story adds a unique thread to the rich tapestry of the sport. These narratives not only inspire but also illuminate the multifaceted nature of female strength – both physical and mental.

The book has delved into various aspects of the sport – training, nutrition, mental health, advocacy, and more. These components are integral to the success and well-being of any athlete. By understanding the scientific principles behind training and nutrition, acknowledging the importance of mental health, and recognizing the power of advocacy and community, female bodybuilders can continue to excel and evolve in their sport.

Looking to the future, women's bodybuilding is poised on the cusp of even greater recognition and development. As stereotypes continue to be dismantled and more women enter the sport, there is a burgeoning sense of opportunity and potential. The increasing visibility and acceptance of female bodybuilders will undoubtedly inspire more women to pursue their strength and fitness goals, whatever they may be.